Walking Inspiration

A 12-Month Plan to Inspire Your Health and Fitness
with 365+ Inspirational Quotes and More

Frank S. Ring
Version 1.0

www.walkingforhealthandfitness.com

March 26, 2020

Published by:

Walking for Health and Fitness
PO Box 1208
Oakland, NJ 07436
www.walkingforhealthandfitness.com

Contents

How to Use this Book

Each month a new topic will be introduced.

Each day of the year will have an inspirational quote related to the monthly topic.

- By tackling each topic on a monthly basis you will be more receptive to the message in each quote and find it easier to gradually implement the quotes and information into your life.
- You can begin this book at anytime of the year. There is no set order in which to apply each monthly lesson.
- I suggest reading each of the monthly **"introductions and lessons"** to get started with a good overview of the book and how to apply it to your life.
- **JUST START NOW!** When I'm at an obstacle in my work, I remind myself to **"just do the next thing."** Anything can be the next thing so just do it!
- Take action, even a small action, and you will begin to get unstuck. I bet when you are stuck, you'll find that, subconsciously, the next action you take will put you on the correct path.
- Trust the process, trust your actions, and believe in yourself! Great things will happen.
- Half way through the month, I'll write more about the topic with more information and to keep you on track.

* * *

Walk on,
Frank Ring

Author: Walking For Health and Fitness
Author: Fitness Walking and Bodyweight Exercises
Website: www.walkingforhealthandfitness.com

Dedication

I proudly dedicate this book to all my high school coaches and teachers. Many of whom I would later call colleagues and friends when I began my second career as a teacher and returned to my alma mater!

Also, to every current and past coaching and teaching colleague for their unending support.

Lastly, to the thousands of students and athletes that have passed through my life.

I hope this book inspires you to walk your way to better health and fitness!

Introduction

Walking Inspiration | A 12 Month Plan to Inspire Your Health and Fitness with 365+ Inspirational Quotes and More

"A year from now you'll wish you started today."
- Karen Lamb

What an exciting time it is right now, in this very moment, to have chosen to read *Walking Inspiration* and to embark on your fitness walking journey!

Walking is the easiest way to get in shape and stay in shape, and with the help of the quotes and information in the book, you will find walking has the power to inspire you to greater wellbeing and accomplishments in your life.

Thoughts, Feelings, and Actions!
These three words will change your life when you apply them. Research has shown on average, people will have **50-70 thousand thoughts per day**.

With this in mind, what are your thoughts:
- Are they negative and filled with dread?
- Are they positive and uplifting?
- Do your thoughts move you to take action?
- Are your thoughts fleeting and all over the place?
- Are you laser focused?

* * *

"The value of an idea lies in the using of it."
- Thomas A. Edison

Your Outer World Reflects Your Inner World.
I put this quote book together as a way to memorialize the
words of some of the greatest minds known to mankind
and to assist you in breaking out of your current mindset
and to get you moving forward, both physically and
mentally.

The key phrase is "moving forward." Yes, walking will
move you forward from one physical place to the next but
the greatest benefit of walking will be moving you from
one emotional place to the next.

Your mindset will dictate where you go, how far you go,
and how much you will enjoy the journey.

Have you ever wondered what the secret is to be
successful in life and in making your dreams come true?

Some people would say that all you need to do is work
very hard to achieve what you want in life. Put your "nose
to the grindstone" and you'll succeed.

Others think that it's all about whom you know and using
that connection to achieve success. "It's not what you
know, it's who you know."

Some feel that there are just people who are "born lucky
and get all the breaks."

* * *

Whatever you believe about success, having a positive mindset is what is going to help you succeed.

This book came about as I began thinking more and more about success. What is it exactly, where can I get some, and how can I apply it so I can lead a better life.

6 Ways Inspirational Quotes Can Change Your Day for the Better

1. **Positive inspirational quotes lessen the impact** of a negative experience. Reading positive inspirational quotes can put things in perspective.
2. **A go-to quote can give you that needed lift.** My mom always used Robert Schuller's quote, "Tough times don't last, but tough people do." She said it so often that I thought she made it up! Let's face it, everyone will face tough times, whether physical, emotional, financial or whatever. For me, having this go-to quote puts the breaks on my negative emotions spinning out of control.
3. **You're not alone:** Inspirational quotes remind us that the thoughts we have are a common experience felt throughout the ages. Your current emotion has been felt, discussed, and written about by others.
4. **Learning opportunities:** There is nothing we can't learn from. Seek out quotes on various topics.
5. **Keep you grounded:** Inspirational quotes give a sense of the greater world around us. The thoughts and ideas of others give us wealth beyond money and bring us back to what is important.
6. **Give perspective:** Picking up from the previous point, inspirational quotes help us get over the

personal setbacks - from illness, loss, or a lack of confidence - we experience from time to time. By making it a habit of reading and writing down your favorite quotes, you can mitigate those downtimes.

How to Use Inspirational Quotes While Walking

- Before your next walk… read the daily quote or pick any quote from the book and … **think on it!**
- Type it into your smartphone notes app and read it back to yourself several times during the walk.
- Record your thoughts and feelings that get inspired by the quote.

You don't need to spend every second of your walk immersed with this quote. I've found that just "putting it out there" in my consciousness will trigger something at some point during the walk.

Often at the very end of the walk, my "breakthrough" insight comes to me. I immediately record my thoughts into my notes app.

"All truly great thoughts are conceived by walking."
- Friedrich Nietzsche

Exclusive Website Resource Page

Download bonus content at:
https://www.walkingforhealthandfitness.com/walking-inspiration-book-resources

- FREE: Audiobook version of *Walking Inspiration | A 12 Month Plan Designed to Inspire Your Health and Fitness with 365+ Quotes and More*
- FREE: *Walking Inspiration* Supplemental Guide
- FREE: *Walking Inspiration*, my quarterly digital magazine.
- FREE: My exclusive *Get Out the Door Checklist* to streamline your walking and fitness routine
- FREE: Additional bonus content will be added throughout the year.

The Walking for Health and Fitness Exercise Principles:

1.   **Work to your fitness level:** increase the intensity as you get stronger
2.   **Be consistent:** avoid long period of inactivity
3.   **Follow an effective routine**
4.   **Set realistic goals:** goals keep you on track
5.   **Record your activities:** keeping a log of your walking miles and fitness routines will keep you motivated when you look back and see just how much you have accomplished
6.   **Make the plan fit your lifestyle**
7.   **Work on your mindset**
8.   **Short bodyweight fitness workouts**(32-minutes is all you need)
9.   **Get inspired:** read uplifting books and listen to audiobooks while you walk
10. **Experiment:** try different things
11. **Make the time:** you don't find time, you make the time to walk
12. **Be patient:** fitness doesn't travel on a straight line
13. **Be happy:** its better than being sad
14. **Reward yourself:** celebrate your accomplishments

Getting in shape is not difficult when you have the right mindset.

Please keep this in mind; you are exercising to get in shape in terms of your cardiovascular system and your muscle strength. Being able to walk for longer periods and increasing your muscle strength will serve you well over the long term, and by long term I mean the rest of your life!

You are not training as if you are an Olympic athlete. If you were training for the Olympics, you would have a training regime that is specific to the event you are competing in. Marathon runners train for miles and miles at a time. Sprinters run shorter, more intense workouts, followed by heavy weight training.

You are training for your own Olympics, the Olympics of the rest of your life. You'll need to be mobile well into advanced age, strong enough to get you to that old age, and most important, if you enjoy the fitness walking process, then it's a win-win.

While all the marathon runners, basketball players, and Boot-camp/Cross-fit devotes are dealing with knee and hip replacement, **you will be walking on!**

January: What's Your Why?

New Year, New You! Where Will You Be One Year From Now?

Wait, Frank, the new year just started and you are asking me about next year already, what's up with that?

It's simple, the calendar turned to the new year and if you are like most people, you will set a new year's resolution, vow to stick to it, then... three weeks from now you are disappointed with yourself because you forgot all about your resolution.

Ask yourself, did you have a game plan? Did you have a written down on paper plan for staying fit in the new year?

So, together we will get you off on the right foot so this year will be your best year ever!

"We are what we think. All that we are arises with our thoughts. With our thoughts, we make the world."
- Budda

What Motivates You?

To get the most from your walking routine, you must know why you want to get into good health and fitness.

Why do you listen to motivational speakers, read motivational quotes and books, and go to motivational seminars? Do these people, literature, and events get you motivated?

Can an expert speaker, or this humble writer, get you out of the house and walking for 30 minutes a day, even in the rain?

Is there something about being motivated that you haven't tapped into yet?

Motivation is defined as the **reason or reasons** one has for acting or behaving in a particular way.

Keep the word reason in mind.

Where Does Motivation Come From?
T. Harv Eker is an author, motivational speaker, and wealth creator. He puts it simply: "Thoughts lead to feelings. Feelings lead to actions. Actions lead to results"!

This got me thinking, is Harv motivating me with his words or is the motivation already within me since it's all about my feelings and actions which both come from within?

What's Your Why?
What is within you that gets you motivated? This is the big question of this January chapter.

Sometimes it's as clear as the nose on your face. The Doctors said if you don't lose weight and get physically fit, your body will continue to break down. That's an easy "why" to answer.

* * *

Fortunately, most of us aren't forced by the diagnosis of impending death to snap us into thinking about what it is that gets us moving towards health and fitness. Most of the time, we just want something in our lives to get us moving and feeling good about ourselves.

Your Dilemma

So, when you are asked, why are you walking? You might just be facing the proverbial chicken and egg situation.

What comes first? Is it knowing the reason you walk or is it I'll get out and walk and my reason will appear?

You might not know your "WHY" at this moment, but I'm here to tell you that walking will give you plenty of time to sort out this "why do I walk" question.

Just do it! Get out on that walk, get into a groove, get lost in your thoughts, and very quickly you will be asking yourself many of life's big questions and pondering the meanings of the quotes in this book.

Now, here is the exciting part, you will quickly come up with answers that you never thought were possible!

Let's face it, if you aren't in shape right now then most likely you haven't yet answered your "WHY" question!

Answer These Four Questions and Get to Your Why:

1. What happens if I don't walk? Write down all the consequences of not being in good shape.

2. What gives me "pep in my step"? What is that one thing

that when you do it, you lose track of time?

3. What are my strengths? We all have strengths and skills. What do you possess that will help you continue walking?

4. What fires up my passion? Walking will give you more time to develop and expand your passion.

Your Next Step:
1. Write down on paper or your Notes App the four questions above then… go out for a walk. That's it. Don't dwell on answering the questions… just let them be and see what happens.

2. Read the daily quote, write it down in a notebook and record what you're thinking about. I use my notes app on my smartphone and record my thoughts while walking.

Download the audiobook version from this book's resource page: https://www.walkingforhealthandfitness.com/walking-inspiration-book-resources

January Quotes

January 1
Walking is man's best medicine.
Hippocrates

Bonus: Start your year off on the right foot (of left if you prefer) but just start! Begin by walking around your block if this is your first walking day. Go longer if you've been walking. No matter the distance, just get out and do it, you know you can!

January 2
The secret of getting ahead is getting started...
Mark Twain

January 3
There is no one giant step that does it. It's a lot of little steps.
Peter A. Cohen

Bonus Quote:
Once you make a decision, the universe conspires to make it happen.
Ralph Waldo Emerson

January 4
Nothing can stop the man with the right mental attitude

from achieving his goal; nothing on earth can help the man with the wrong mental attitude.
Thomas Jefferson

January 5
Nothing in this world can take the place of persistence. Talent will not; nothing is more common than unsuccessful men with talent. Genius will not; unrewarded genius is almost a proverb. Education will not; the world is full of educated derelicts. Persistence and determination alone are omnipotent.
Calvin Coolidge

January 6
A vigorous five-mile walk will do more good for an unhappy but otherwise healthy adult than all the medicine and psychology in the world.
Paul Dudley White

January 7
Try and fail, but don't fail to try.
John Quincy Adams

January 8
As I grow older, I pay less attention to what men say. I just watch what they do.
Andrew Carnegie

January 9
For success, attitude is equally as important as ability.
Walter Scott

* * *

January 10

Our greatest enemies, the ones we must fight most often,
are within…

Thomas Paine

January 11

Between stimulus and response, there is a space. In that
space is our power to choose our response. In our response
lies our growth and our freedom.

Victor Frankl

January 12

You will never do anything in this world without courage.
It is the greatest quality of the mind next to honor.

Aristotle

January 13

I'm a great believer in luck, and I find the harder I work,
the more I have of it…

Thomas Jefferson

January 14

Be kind for everyone is fighting a hard battle.

Neil Peart

January 15

Mid-month Point to Ponder:

Have you found your why yet? If so, congratulations!
You've set yourself up for success in your walking for
health and fitness program.

If you haven't, keep exploring why you want to continue

walking and getting fit. Trust me, the answer will come to you during a walk.

Ask yourself the question beforehand, type it into your notes app and **"think on it!"**

"What the mind of man can conceive and believe, it can achieve."
Napoleon Hill

January 16
I just love when people say I can't do something because all my life people said I wasn't going to make it.
Ted Turner

January 17
You will never find time for anything. You must make it.
Charles Buxton

January 18
Some of us have great runways already built for us. If you have one, take off. But if you don't have one, realize it is your responsibility to grab a shovel and build one for yourself and for those who will follow after you.
Amelia Earhart

January 19
The Strongest principle of growth lies in human choice.
George Eliot

January 20
Work like you don't need the money. Love like you've

never been hurt. Dance like nobody is watching.
Mark Twain

January 21
The more steps people take during the day, the better their moods. Why? Walking! It releases natural, feel-good, pain-killing endorphins into your body.
Frank Ring

January 22
Success is never ending, failure is never final.
Dr. Robert Schuller

January 23
Knowing is not enough; we must apply. Willing is not enough; we must do.
Johann Wolfgang von Goethe

January 24
When you arise in the morning, think of what a precious privilege it is to be alive. To breathe, to think, to enjoy, to love.
Marcus Aurelius

January 25
The mind is not a vessel to be filled but a fire to be kindled.
Plutarch

January 26
Well done is better than well said.
Benjamin Franklin

* * *

January 27
A mind that is stretched by a new experience can never go back to its old dimensions.
Oliver Wendell Holmes, Jr.

January 28
Our greatest enemies, the ones we must fight most often, are within…
Thomas Paine

January 29
If your actions inspire others to dream more, learn more, do more and become more, you are a leader.
John Quincy Adams

January 30
Everybody needs beauty as well as bread, places to play in and pray in, where nature may heal and give strength to body and soul alike.
John Muir

January 31
The future belongs to those who believe in the beauty of their dreams.
Eleanor Roosevelt

"You can't make positive choices for the rest of your life without an environment that makes those choices easy, natural, and enjoyable."
Deepak Chopra

February: Setting Goals

If you don't know your destination, any road will take you there.

This month, let's focus on your goals:
- How you can set them
- How you'll use them to motivate yourself
- How you will write them down on paper and read them often

"By recording your dreams and goals on paper, you set in motion the process of becoming the person you most want to be. Put your future in good hands—your own."
- Mark Victor Hansen

Developing a fitness routine is a major undertaking. Like and archer aiming for the target, having a destination to aim for will keep you on track to reach the health and fitness level you'd like to achieve.

Don't confuse having a wish with having a goal
Most people think that having a vague idea of what they want and being positive and optimistic about accomplishing it is a goal. This isn't for you!

Only 3 percent of people have clear, written goals with plans to accomplish them. Only 3 percent of people work on their most important goals each day.

You want to be among the 3 percent!

"If you want a happy life, tie it to goals, not people or things."
- Albert Einstein

Goal Setting Made Simple
Before you actually "walk" to your goal, you need to take a series of planning steps to dramatically increase the chances that you will be successful.

Seven Step to Setting Your New Exciting Goals:
1. Decide exactly what you want in terms of health and fitness
2. Write down your goals and make them measurable
3. Set a deadline
4. Identify all the obstacles that you will have to overcome to achieve your goals
5. Determine the additional knowledge and skills that you will require to achieve your goals
6. Determine those people whose help and cooperation you will require to achieve your goals
7. Make a list of all your answers to the above, and organize them by sequence and priority

By following these seven steps, you can accomplish any goal that you set for yourself.

Your Next Step
Set 2 goals for yourself:
- **Set one big long-term goal:** Give yourself a compelling reason to get up and walk each day.
- **Set one small goal that you can accomplish today:** We all need a win every day!

As you walk, use the time to focus on your main goal. How will you feel when you accomplish it? What does it taste like, smell like, look like?

Read the daily quotes: use them to fuel you towards your goals.

"If you aim for nothing, you'll hit it every time."
– Source unknown

February: Setting Goals

February 1
Begin with the end in mind.
Stephen Covey

February 2
If one advances confidently in the direction of his dreams, and endeavors to live the life which he has imagined, he will meet with a success unexpected in common hours.
Henry David Thoreau

February 3
One way to keep momentum going is to have constantly greater goals.
Michael Korda

February 4
Obstacles are those frightful things you can see when you take your eyes off your goal.
Henry Ford

February 5
You measure the size of the accomplishment by the obstacles you had to overcome to reach your goals.
Booker T. Washington

* * *

February 6
Success is the progressive realization of worthwhile, predetermined, personal goals.
Paul J. Meyer

February 7
I only went out for a walk, and finally concluded to stay out till sundown, for going out, I found, was really going in.
John Muir

February 8
People with goals succeed because they know where they're going.
Earl Nightingale

February 9
If you go to work on your goals, your goals will go to work on you. If you go to work on your plan, your plan will go to work on you. Whatever good things we build end up building us.
Jim Rohn

February 10
Give me a stock clerk with a goal and I'll give you a man who will make history. Give me a man with no goals and I'll give you a stock clerk.
J.C. Penney

February 11
In every walk with nature one receives far more than he seeks.

John Muir

February 12
Goals are dreams we convert to plans and take action to fulfill.
Zig Ziglar

February 13
We must walk consciously only part way toward our goal, and then leap in the dark to our success.
Henry David Thoreau

February 14
Success equals goals... all else is commentary.
Brian Tracy

February 15
Mid-month Point to Ponder
- Are your goals written down?
- Do you read your goals several times a day?
- Have you taken action to progress towards your most important goal today?

Here is a great technique to help you reach your goals. Every morning before doing anything else, open a notebook and **write down your main goal ten times.** Do this every morning to keep your main goal in front of you as you start your day.

"Man is a goal-seeking animal. His life only has meaning if he is reaching out and striving for his goals."
Aristotle

"Most impossible goals can be met simply by breaking them down into bite size chunks, writing them down, believing them and going full speed ahead as if they were routine."
Don Lancaster

February 16
Every ceiling, when reached, becomes a floor, upon which one walks as a matter of course and prescriptive right.
Aldous Huxley

February 17
Reach high, for stars lie hidden in your soul. Dream deep, for every dream precedes the goal.
Pamela Vaull Star

February 18
You should set goals beyond your reach so you always have something to live for.
Ted Turner

February 19
The greater danger for most of us isn't that our aim is too high and miss it, but that it is too low and we reach it.
Michelangelo

* * *

February 20
In the absence of clearly defined goals, we become strangely loyal to performing daily acts of trivia.
Author Unknown

February 21
The trouble with not having a goal is that you can spend your life running up and down the field and never score.
Bill Copeland

February 22
If you're bored with life – you don't get up every morning with a burning desire to do things – you don't have enough goals.
Lou Holtz

February 23
Setting goals is the first step in turning the invisible into the visible.
Tony Robbins

February 24
If you want to be happy, set a goal that commands your thoughts, liberates your energy and inspires your hopes.
Andrew Carnegie

February 25
It must be borne in mind that the tragedy of life doesn't lie in not reaching your goal. The tragedy lies in having no goals to reach.
Benjamin E. Mays

* * *

February 26
Goals are the fuel in the furnace of achievement.
Brian Tracy

February 27
Envision, create, and believe in your own universe, and the universe will form around you.
Tony Hsieh

February 28
Discipline is the bridge between goals and accomplishment.
Jim Rohn

February 29 (Leap Year)
Your goal should be just out of reach, but not out of sight.
Denis Waitley and Remi Witt

"A goal properly set is halfway reached."
Zig Zigler

March: Benefits of Walking

Why Walking?
Walking is the easiest way to get in shape and stay in shape! I began walking after a back injury forced me out of work for four months. During my recovery, I discovered that by walking, I felt great physically and mentally.

Much like the effects of meditation, **walking expanded time**. My mind wandered, my body moved to an internal beat, and I was healing.

Walking as little as 30-minutes a day at a comfortable pace has been shown to:
- Reduce the risks of heart disease
- Increase stamina
- Improve overall health
- Reduce stress
- Improve self-esteem and mood

Pleasure Walking
Pleasure walking is the "everyday" type of walking you do all day. Walking to your car, walking into your place of work, or walking downstairs to your living room.

Think of the campaign to walk 10,000 steps per day. Pleasure walking is a good beginner level, which will build stamina and strength. The focus of this level is your long-term health and improved quality of life.

* * *

When you are pleasure walking, you can generally walk a mile between 17-24 minutes.

"If you don't like the road you're walking, start paving another one."
- Dolly Parton

How Much Should You Walk?
The key will be to focus on consistency rather than intensity. I recommend 30 to 60 minutes of walking per day on most days of the week.

You don't have to do the walks all at one time. Several mini-walks are just as effective as one long walk.

Ideas to get in more walking time:
- Walk in the morning, at lunchtime, and dinnertime for at least 10 minutes or more.
- Walk to a local destination instead of driving.
- Park your car a few blocks from your job or other destination.
- Window-shop at the mall.
- Schedule 20-30 minute sessions on a treadmill if you have access to one.

How-to Determine Intensity
Remember, my goal here is to get you out and walking; you don't need to know these numbers to enjoy walking, but knowledge is power so with that said, let's see how you can measure intensity.

* * *

Pleasure walking should feel like a 3-5 on a scale of 1-10. Only you can determine your rate of perceived exertion.

Talk Test
An excellent gauge of walking intensity is how difficult it is to carry on a conversation. When pleasure walking, you should be able to carry on a reasonable conversation while walking.

Walking Form:
- Head up and centered
- Shoulders back
- Chest naturally lifted
- Arms low and slightly bent
- Hands loosely cupped
- Abdominals: belly button pulled towards the spine
- Hips loose and natural
- Thighs: natural movement; a link between your hips and lower leg
- Feet: heels strike the ground first
- Breathing and heart rate – Keep breathing smoothly, deeply, and regularly. By breathing in a relaxed manner your heart will beat steadily and rhythmically

Your Next Step
Walk, walk, walk! Try not to go more than 2 days in a row without going out for a walk.

"Our first steps are among the most celebrated milestones of our youth.
But for some reason, as we age, walking gets taken for

*granted.
That's puzzling since walking is one of the most comprehensive
and safest fitness routines available.
All you need is a good pair of walking shoes and socks,
and you are good to go."*
- BRION O'CONNOR

March: Benefits of Walking

March 1
From the child's first faltering step across the homely
carpet, to the astronaut's "one giant stride for mankind"
over the alien moon dust, walking is the simplest but most
glorious declaration of human independence.
Duncan Minshull

March 2
Walking brings me back to myself.
Laurette Mortimer

March 3
A morning walk gives the body a chance to forgive the
trials and tribulations of yesterday, to shed its rubbish and
mental clutter.
Terri Guillemets

March 4
Walking is the best possible exercise. Habituate yourself to
walk very fast.
Thomas Jefferson

March 5
I am alarmed when it happens that I have walked a mile
into the woods bodily, without getting there in spirit.
Henry David Thoreau

* * *

March 6

If I am walking with two other men, each of them will serve as my teacher. I will pick out the good points of the one and imitate them, and the bad points of the other and correct them in myself.
Confucius

March 7

Walking with a friend in the dark is better than walking alone in the light.
Helen Keller

March 8

All truly great thoughts are conceived by walking.
Friedrich Nietzsche

March 9

Everywhere is within walking distance if you have the time.
Steven Wright

March 10

The happiest moments are when we sit down and we feel the presence of our brothers and sisters, lay and monastic, who are practicing walking and sitting mediation.
Thich Nhat Hanh

March 11

Beauty surrounds us, but usually we need to be walking in a garden to know it.
Rumi

* * *

March 12

I walk every day, and I look at the mountains and the fields and the small city, and I say: 'Oh my God, what a blessing.' Then you realize it's important to put it in a context beyond this woman, this man, this city, this country, this universe.
Paulo Coelho

March 13

It's your road, and yours alone. Others may walk it with you, but no one can walk it for you.
Rumi

March 14

The higher we are placed, the more humbly we should walk.
Marcus Tullius Cicero

March 15

Mid-month Point to Ponder

THERE ARE SO MANY THINGS TO DO WHILE WALKING!

It was a pleasure to come up with the top 29 things to do while walking. I've done all of them and they've kept me walking, entertained, and in great shape!

It's a funny thing when I tell people I enjoy walking, they tell me it's so boring. Quite honestly, I don't get that. I've found so many things to do while walking.

"The best way to lengthen out our days is to walk steadily and with a purpose."
Charles Dickens

"If you seek creative ideas go walking. Angels whisper to a man when he goes for a walk."
Raymond Inmon

"An early morning walk is a blessing for the whole day."
Henry David Thoreau

March 16
But the beauty is in the walking -- we are betrayed by destinations.
Gwyn Thomas

March 17
There comes . . . a longing never to travel again except on foot.
Wendell Berry

March 18
When real people fall down in life, they get right back up and keep on walking.
Michael Patrick King

March 19
Walking is the only form of transportation in which a man proceeds erect, like a man, on his own legs, under his own

power. There is immense satisfaction in that.
Edward Abbey

March 20
If I could not walk far and fast, I think I should just
explode and perish.
Charles Dickens

March 21
I like long walks, especially when they are taken by people
who annoy me.
Noel Coward

March 22
Walk as if you are kissing the Earth with your feet.
Thich Nhat Hanh

March 23
Go back to what's good, what's certain, what's always
there. You woke up today. Just start walking.
Jesse L. Martin

March 24
Above all, do not lose your desire to walk. Every day I
walk myself into a state of well-being and walk away from
every illness. I have walked myself into my best thoughts,
and I know of no thought so burdensome that one cannot
walk away from it.
Soren Kierkegaard

March 25
Walking is the do anywhere, anytime, no-instruction-

needed exercise.
Brion O'Connor

March 26

On your deathbed, will you wish you'd spent more prime weekend hours grocery shopping or walking in the woods with your kids?
Louise Lague

March 27

The best remedy for a short temper is a long walk.
Jacqueline Schiff

March 28

Walking is a technique of solitude, a way into reverie. The walker is not a sleepwalker but a daydreamer.
Deirdre Heddon

March 28

Walking is a year-round activity, and need not be confined to the dry summer months, for there is as much beauty to be found in the countryside in the leafless months of winter as in vibrant spring and the golden days of autumn.
Kev Reynolds

March 30

Although there are many ways to achieve a healthier lifestyle, walking is proven to have the highest success rate because people are less likely to quit doing it than with other physical activities.
Samantha Morgan

* * *

March 31

There is no one giant step that does it. It's a lot of little steps.

Peter A. Cohen

Do you like this book?

Please write a review. Go to the resource page:
www.walkingforhealthandfitness.com/walking-inspiration-book-resources

...Thank you!

"Walking for health and fitness, the easiest way to get in shape and stay in shape."
Frank Ring

April: Supercharge Your Fitness

Benefits of Performing Bodyweight Exercises While Walking.

It seemed simple to me that while I was out on my walks I felt I needed to exercise my whole body.

I loved walking and loved being in shape, but I didn't like working out in my home gym. When I went to my basement gym I very rarely was psyched up to work out. My motivation ranged from "let me get through this as quickly as possible, too... how much can I procrastinate between sets?"

When I was in the gym I wanted to be outdoors, moving, seeing things, thinking, daydreaming and creating. The home gym restricted this.

Then the lightbulb went off... **work out while walking!**

It makes total sense as you are always with your body, so your gym is available to you anywhere at any time 24/7. You are limited only by your imagination.

> *"Let your body be your exercise machine."*
> *-Robert Boggs*

Bodyweight Exercises Rely on Natural Motion and are Functional.

For instance, pushups mimic the motion of pushing a piece of furniture across the room when you need to move it to redecorate or vacuum. You must tighten your core muscles, then engage your hips, legs, and upper body.

In contrast, laying on a bench and pushing up a barbell full of weights do not give you the same functional workout.

You need to move your body throughout the day and bodyweight exercises strengthen you for day-to-day activities!

Through bodyweight exercises you will develop greater body strength, muscular and cardiovascular endurance, flexibility, increased walking speed, and improved coordination.

Performing bodyweight exercises while walking will allow you to achieve continuous positive results and greater body control. You will gain time by not having to travel to a gym and you will save money as walking and doing **bodyweight exercises are FREE.**

Promotes "Youth Hormones"
An effective strength training regimen promotes the release of vital "youth" hormones:

- Testosterone (for men)
- Estradiol and Estrogen (for women)

Strength training helps prevent the loss of muscular

strength known to accompany aging.

They're Free
When I say, "strength-training", I don't mean heading to the gym and using stationary machines. Your body weight is all you need to get these fantastic benefits.

Bodyweight exercise develops functional strength. This is the strength you need to go about your daily life.

Improves Your Balance and Flexibility
Bodyweight training engages your core muscles and improves strength in your limbs.

More than one-third of persons 65 years of age or older fall each year, and in half of such cases, the falls are recurrent. Falls are the main cause of morbidity and disability in the elderly.

Variety
You have so many choices of exercises. Change it up every workout to tone your whole body.

Change the locations in which to work out. On a beautiful fall day head to a park and enjoy the leaves changing colors. Hot summer day… get to the beach and workout along the shoreline.

"HIIT" – High-Intensity Interval Training"
The HIIT exercises allow you to activate more muscles during your workouts, burn more calories while you work out, and keep burning calories (and activating your cells'

mitochondria) after you're done working out.

HIIT training is doing a bodyweight exercise for a specific amount of time.

For example: walk for 4 minutes, then stop and do push-ups for 30-40 seconds. Then resume walking for another 4 minutes, then do 30-40 seconds of push-ups.

Quick and to the Point

Quick sets of bodyweight exercises have been proven to contribute to weight loss more effectively than long cardio sessions. The results of bodyweight exercises are a lean, fit, and strong body.

As you'll see, you can change the intensity of the exercises at any time by adjusting how the exercise is performed:

- Leverage
- Using an unstable platform
- Pausing during the exercise
- The number of points of contact
- Range of motion
- Speed

Bodyweight Exercise List:*

- Push-ups
- Squats
- Lunges
- Planks

Your Next Step

1. Begin performing bodyweight exercises during your walks.

2. Download the list of bodyweight exercises from the resource page.

*Download the Supplemental Guide for this book at the https://www.walkingforhealthandfitness.com/walking-inspiration-book-resources

April: Supercharge Your Fitness

April 1
You're only one workout away from a good mood.
Unknown

April 2
It's going to be a journey. It's not a sprint to get in shape.
Kerri Walsh Jennings

April 3
All great achievements require time.
Maya Angelou

April 4
No matter how many mistakes you make or how slow you progress, you are still way ahead of everyone who isn't trying.
Tony Robbins

April 5
Just believe in yourself. Even if you don't pretend that you do and, and some point, you will.
Venus Williams

April 6
Today I will do what others won't, so tomorrow I can accomplish what others can't.
Jerry Rice

* * *

April 7
Do something today that your future self will thank you for.
Unknown

April 8
We are what we repeatedly do. Excellence then is not an act but a habit.
Aristotle

April 9
Strive for progress, not perfection.
Unknown

April 10
No matter how slow you go, you are still lapping everybody on the couch.
Unknown

April 11
You miss 100% of the shots you don't take.
Wayne Gretzky

April 12
The difference between the impossible and the possible lies in a person's determination.
Tommy Lasorda

April 13
If you want something you've never had, you must be willing to do something you've never done.
Thomas Jefferson

* * *

April 14
To give anything less than your best is to sacrifice the gift.
Steve Prefontaine

April 15
Mid-month Point to Ponder
How to get more fitness into your walks.
- Lacking motivation to get out the door and walk?
- Are you walking already but feel stagnated?
- Are you looking for new inspiration in the changing of the season?

Whatever your situation, reading words of wisdom from successful people can be super-inspiring.

With that in mind, keep up your daily reading of these amazing motivational quotes from notable figures to help you kick start your walking routine and inspire you to reach your fitness goals.

"I've missed more than 9,000 shots in my career. I've lost almost 300 games. Twenty-six times I've been trusted to take the game-winning shot and missed. I've failed over and over and over again in my life. And that is why I succeed."
Michael Jordan

April 16
Strength does not come from physical capacity. It comes from an indomitable will.
Mahatma Gandhi

April 17
The difference between try and triumph is a little 'umph'.
Unknown

April 18
Don't count the days, make the days count.
Muhammad Ali

April 19
Sweat is fat crying.
Unknown

April 20
Nothing will work unless you do.
Maya Angelou

April 21
Making excuses burns zero calories per hour.
Unknown

April 22
Don't let the scale define you. Be active, be healthy, be happy.
Unknown

* * *

April 23
Success usually comes to those who are too busy to be looking for it.
Henry David Thoreau

April 24
All progress takes place outside the comfort zone.
Michael John Bobak

April 25
The only place where success comes before work is in the dictionary.
Vidal Sassoon

April 26
The clock is ticking. Are you becoming the person you want to be?
Greg Plitt

April 27
We cannot start over. But we can begin now and make a new ending.
Zig Ziglar

April 28
You must expect great things of yourself before you can do them.
Michael Jordan

April 29
Action is the foundational key to all success.
Pablo Picasso

* * *

April 30
If something stands between you and your success, move
it. Never be denied.
Dwayne 'The Rock' Johnson

"It is never too late to be what you might have been."
George Eliot

May: Tracking Your Progress

In March, I detailed the benefits of walking, in April I detailed the benefits of doing bodyweight exercises to supercharge your fitness. Now, let's focus on why you must log your walking and fitness exercises.

Benefits of Logging and Tracking Your Walking Progress
By recording your walking mileage, steps, and the exercises you do during your walks, you will gain a wealth of knowledge about your progress.

Progress is defined as a forward or onward movement towards a destination. May these quotes inspire you to keep making progress in the direction of your dreams.

When I look back over at my walking logs* I get a great overview of the work I've put into my fitness. The training log adds a great boost to my motivation when I see, on paper or spreadsheet, just how far my fitness walking has progressed. I clearly see my progress from the time I started recovering from my back injury and could only walk down the block and back to doing long walks of over ten miles!

"A little progress every day adds up to big results."
- Satya
* * *

You've put in the work on a consistent basis and you've developed a routine that is efficient and effective. You can walk more miles per day then you thought you'd ever walk. That is awesome... If I was with you, I'd pat you on the back, but that's not possible so do the next best thing...

Pat yourself on the back as you see just how much improvement you've made to your health and fitness!

"Make measurable progress in reasonable time."
- Jim Rohn

Tracking Your Bodyweight Fitness Exercises Will Motivate You
Strength workouts compliment your walks and have incredible benefits that will make you a better walker.

Log your workouts by noting how many pushups, squats, lunges, and planks you can do comfortably, and go from there. Are you able to complete two more pushups after a week? Plank for 10 or 20 more seconds? Then write it down and celebrate!

Regularly tracking your workout progress is important for several reasons:
1. Makes it more likely to reach and surpass your goal
2. Allows you to be more efficient with your time and workouts
3. Lends accountability to yourself and your goals
4. Allows for easier modifications and shows when and where changes need to be mad
5. Can be motivating and reinforcing to remind you

        why you are doing what you are doing

6.   Helps to drive the focus and direction of your Fitness program
7.   Keeps you committed to your plan
8.   You see your progress!

Your Next Step:
As you develop your strength training routine, keep a log of your progress. Keep the routine simple at first then, as you get stronger, add more elements to your routine.

"Small progress is still progress."
Frank S. Ring

May: Tracking Your Progress

May 1
Progress lies not in enhancing what is, but in advancing toward what will be.
Khalil Gibran

May 2
We all want progress, but if you're on the wrong road, progress means doing an about-turn and walking back to the right road; in that case, the man who turns back soonest is the most progressive.
C. S. Lewis

May 3
Without deviation from the norm, progress is not possible.
Frank Zappa

May 4
You don't make progress by standing on the sidelines, whimpering and complaining. You make progress by implementing ideas.
Shirley Chisholm

May 5
True progress quietly and persistently moves along without notice.
St. Francis of Assisi

* * *

May 6
Make measurable progress in reasonable time.
Jim Rohn

May 7
Progress is measured by richness and intensity of experience - by a wider and deeper apprehension of the significance and scope of human existence.
Herbert Read

May 8
Everybody's a work in progress. I'm a work in progress. I mean, I've never arrived... I'm still learning all the time.
Renee Fleming

May 9
If progress is to be steady we must have long term guides extending far ahead.
Dwight D. Eisenhower

May 10
Progress always involves risks. You can't steal second base and keep your foot on first.
Frederick Wilcox

May 11
When any real progress is made, we unlearn and learn anew what we thought we knew before.
Henry David Thoreau

May 12
If there is no struggle, there is no progress.

Frederick Douglass

May 13
Passion. Purpose. Progress.
Anonymous

May 14
Courage means to keep making forward progress while you still feel afraid.
Joyce Meyer

May 15
Mid-month Point to Ponder
If you haven't done so yet, create a log to track your fitness progress!

By tracking your progress you will get to know your health and fitness level. As your walking speed increases, you will feel great knowing you are taking control of your wellbeing.

Regularly tracking your workout progress makes it more likely to reach and surpass your goals. It keeps you committed to your plan and you'll see your improvement!

"Human progress is neither automatic nor inevitable. Every step toward the goals requires sacrifice, suffering, and struggle; the tireless exertions and passionate concern of dedicated individuals."
Martin Luther King
* * *

"Little by little becomes a lot."
Anonymous

"Consider what a long way you've come."
Anonymous

May 16
Progress is impossible without change, and those who cannot change their minds cannot change anything.
George Bernard Shaw

May 17
Strive for progress, not perfection.
Anonymous

May 18
Don't compare your progress to that of others. We need our own time to travel our own distance.
Anonymous

May 19
Always be a work in progress.
Emily Lillian

May 20
Slow, steady progress is better than daily excuses.
Robin Sharma

May 21
Success is steady progress toward one's personal goals.
Jim Rohn

* * *

May 22
Work hard for you and your own goals. Progress will come.
Anonymous

May 23
Progress is not inevitable. It's up to us to create it.
Anonymous

May 24
Allow yourself to be proud of yourself and all the progress you've made. Especially the progress that no one else can see.
Anonymous

May 25
Comfort is the enemy of progress.
P. T. Barnum

May 26
Never discourage anyone who continually makes progress, no matter how slow.
Plato

May 27
Some quit due to slow progress. Never grasping the fact that slow progress is progress.
Jeff Olson

May 28
A lack of focus leads to a lack of progress. Focus. Grind. Grow.
Anonymous

* * *

May 29
Whatever you do you have to keep moving forward.
Martin Luther King

May 30
The moment a man ceases to progress, to grow higher,
wider and deeper, then his life becomes stagnant.
Orison S. Marden

May 31
Without continual growth and progress, such words as
improvement, achievement, and success have no meaning.
Benjamin Franklin

"There are only two options: Make progress or make
excuses."
Anonymous

June: The Power of Your Breath

Your breath, more specifically your breathing, is a powerful weapon in your healthcare arsenal. Far too many people zone out in front of the TV after a stressful day as a way to "relax", but this will not activate the body's *Natural Relaxation Response.*

You might be thinking, "Frank, isn't sitting, resting, and watching a ball game a way to relieve stress? It's what I always do." Well, the quick answer is it might help but in fact, what you need to do is activate your body's *Natural Relaxation Response.*

"But if we go beyond our mind, breathing can open up a completely new foundation for our life."
—ILSA MIDDENDORF

Don't be fooled by the term "relaxation" as it has a different meaning in this case. The *Relaxation Response* is a physical state of deep rest that changes the physical and emotional responses to stress leading to decreased heart rate, reduced blood pressure, a slower rate of breathing, and an easing of muscle tension.

You trigger the relaxation response by abdominal breathing for 20-30 minutes per day. Yes, you can lay down in front of your TV and do the deep breathing exercises, or you can supercharge your deep breathing by fitness walking.

The act of walking is as natural as breathing. Breathing is something we can control and regulate. It is a useful tool for achieving a relaxed and clear state of mind.

I will show you how proper breathing while walking will help you gain the full benefits of walking.

"Deep breaths are like little love notes to your body."
- Unknown

To Breathe Properly, You Need to:
   • Breathe deeply into your abdomen, not just your chest.
   • Breathing exercises should be deep, slow, rhythmic, and in through the nose, out through the mouth.
   • The most important part of deep breathing is to regulate your breaths.

I use an odd number pattern to my breathing routine. The pattern is based on the number of steps you choose to count. The idea is that by using an odd number, the cycle will repeat itself on the opposite foot each time.

Odd Number Breathing Pattern:
   • Begin by inhaling through your nose thereby expanding the belly for 4 steps
   • Then, exhale through your mouth, for 3 steps (pulling your abs in)
   • Repeat the cycle 4 in, 3 out
   • The cycle is 7 steps (an odd number).

• Adjust the pattern as you see fit, but always use an odd number with the inhale 1 step more than the exhale.

Going forward, if you need to shorten the count - especially if breathing gets heavier with more exertion - just change to 5 steps; 3 steps inhale, 2 steps exhale.

Walking and Breathing:
When we use the Odd Number Breathing Cycle, the cycle alternates the start point (or foot we land on) with each cycle of breathing.

Example:
*   **First step (left foot)** breathe in
*   Second step (right foot) breathe in
*   Third step (left foot) breathe in
*   Forth step (right foot) breathe in
*   Fifth step (left foot) breathe OUT
*   Sixth step (right foot) breathe OUT
*   Seventh step (left foot) breathe OUT

Repeat the cycle. Notice that the first step changes to start on your right foot!
*   **First step (Right foot)** breathe in
*   Second step (left foot) breathe in
*   Third step (right foot) breathe in
*   And so on, and so on…

As you can see, by walking you are **RELAXING!**

Benefits of Walking to Activate the Relaxation Response:
*   Metabolism decreases

- Slower heartbeat
- Muscle relaxation
- Slower breathing
- Increases levels of nitric oxide which is a vasodilator, meaning it relaxes the inner muscles of your blood vessels causing them to widen. This increases blood flow and lowers blood pressure.

When you can't walk, schedule your deep breathing exercise just as you would schedule important business appointments. Set aside a minimum of two 5-minute segments of time every day to just sit and deep breathe using the **Odd Number Breathing Pattern.**

"Breathe, believe, receive"
-Frank Ring

Your Next Step:
Begin using the **Odd Number Breathing Pattern** on your next walk. Start slowly and do it for a few minutes at a time several times throughout your walk.

As you gain walking experience, you will find yourself effortlessly slipping into this breathing pattern. Also, set aside time each day to sit and do the deep breathing exercises.

"Breath is Spirit. The act of breathing is Living."
Author Unknown

June: The Power of Your Breath

June 1
Remember, as long as you are breathing it's never too late to start a new beginning.
Author Unknown

June 2
Breathing is the greatest pleasure in life.
Giovanni Papini

June 3
Breathing affects your respiratory, cardiovascular, neurological, gastrointestinal, muscular, and psychic systems, and also has a general effect on your sleep, memory, ability to concentrate, and your energy levels.
Donna Farhi

June 4
Breath is the bridge which connects life to consciousness, which unites your body to your thoughts.
Thích Nhất Hạnh

June 5
Breathe. Let go. And remind yourself that this very moment is the only one you know you have for sure.
Oprah Winfrey

June 6
Inhale the future, exhale the past.

Author Unknown

June 7
Breathe deeply, until sweet air extinguishes the burn of fear in your lungs and every breath is a beautiful refusal to become anything less than infinite.
D. Antoinette Foy

June 8
When the breath is unsteady, all is unsteady; when the breath is still; all is still. Control the breath carefully. Inhalation gives strength and a controlled body; retention gives steadiness of mind and longevity; exhalation purifies body and spirit.
Goraksasathakam

June 9
The wisest one-word sentence? Breathe.
Terri Guillemets

June 10
If you woke up breathing, congratulations! You have another chance.
Andrea Boydston

June 11
Breathe in deeply to bring your mind home to your body.
Thich Nhat Hanh

June 12
Breathe, it's just a bad day, not a bad life.
Author Unknown

* * *

June 13
Whenever I feel blue, I start breathing again.
L. Frank Baum

June 14
Just breathing can be such a luxury at times.
Author unknown

June 15
Mid-month Point to Ponder
To breathe properly, you need to breathe deeply into your abdomen, not just your chest. Breathing exercises should be deep, slow, rhythmic, and in through the nose, out through the mouth. The most important part of deep breathing is to regulate your breaths.

I use an odd number pattern to my breathing routine.

Odd Number Breathing Pattern: 7-Step Cycle
- Begin by inhaling through your nose thereby expanding the belly for 4 steps
- Then, exhale through your mouth, for 3 steps (pulling your abs in)
- Repeat the cycle 4 in, 3 out
- The cycle is 7 steps (an odd number).
- Adjust the pattern as you see fit, but always use an odd number with your inhale 1 step more than your exhale.

Going forward, if you need to shorten the count, especially if breathing gets heavier with more exertion-- just change to 5 steps; 3 steps inhale, 2 steps exhale.

Walking and Breathing: When we use the Odd Number Breathing Cycle, the cycle alternates the start point (or foot we land on) with each cycle of breathing.

"Improper breathing is a common cause of ill health."
- Dr. Andrew Weil

"Breathing is meditation; life is a meditation. You have to breathe in order to live, so breathing is how you get in touch with the sacred space of your heart."
- Willow Smith

"For breath is life, so if you breathe well you will live long on earth."
- Sanskrit Proverb

June 16
Conscious breathing heightens awareness and deepens relaxation.
Dan Brule

June 17
Smile, breathe, take it slow, and live a happy life.
Johnny Lung

June 18
Breath is the link between mind and body.
Dan Brule

* * *

June 19
Life isn't measured by the number of breaths we take, but by the moments that take our breath away.
Author Unknown

June 20
Breathing, according to me, corresponds to taking charge of one's own life.
Luce Irigaray

June 21
Feelings come and go like clouds in a windy sky. Conscious breathing is my anchor.
Thich Nhat Hanh

June 22
I wake up every day and think, "I'm breathing! It's a good day."
Eve Ensler

June 23
Breathing well means breathing more slowly and deeply. Relax, feel your breathing, and breathe comfortably. Once aware, it naturally becomes deeper and slower.
Ilchi Lee

June 24
There is one way of breathing that is shameful and constricted. Then there's another way; a breath of love that takes you all the way to infinity.
Rumi

* * *

June 25
Breathing control gives man strength, vitality, inspiration, and magic powers.
Zhuangzi

June 26
Breathing in, I calm body and mind. Breathing out, I smile. Dwelling in the present moment, I know this is the only moment.
Thich Nhat Hanh

June 27
I love to breathe. Oxygen is sexy!
Kris Carr

June 28
Listen. Are you breathing just a little and calling it a life?
Mary Oliver

June 29
Focusing on the act of breathing clears the mind of all daily distractions and clears our energy enabling us to better connect with the Spirit within.
Author Unknown

June 30
Every day is a new beginning. Take a deep breath. Smile, and start again.
Author Unknown

"As you waste your breath complaining about life, someone out there is breathing their last. Appreciate what you have."
Author Unknown

July: Walking Speed: Take More STEPS to Live Longer

Do you want to live longer? Enjoy a healthier and more productive life? Save money and feel better than you have in your entire life?

New research has revealed that average walking speed can be a useful indicator of life expectancy and, as you'll learn, there are five specific steps you can take to increase your average walking speed.

Average Walking Speed Predicts Life Expectancy of Older Adults

Average walking speed is a powerful indicator of vitality. Average walking speed studies show that an older person's pace, along with their age and gender, can predict their life expectancy just as well as the complex battery of other health indicators such as blood pressure, body mass index, chronic conditions, and smoking history.

Older adults that were able to walk 2.25 miles per hour or faster consistently lived longer than others within their age group. Very simply put, a person's capacity to move strongly reflects their health and vitality.

"The real pride, the real present, is your health and longevity."
-Richard Simmons

* * *

How to Increase Your Average Walking Speed

Increase your average walking speed by thinking "S.T.E.P.S"!

Having this simple mental device to remind you of what you need to do will get you moving quickly with just a little practice.

On Your Next Walk Apply "STEPS":

Shorter quicker strides:

Turnover rate is the key to quicker walking. The more steps you take per minute, the quicker you will walk. Think of a car's piston pumping up and down quickly. You may think that a longer stride would help you walk faster but this is not the case. Increasing your stride puts your legs in an outstretched position which acts as a break. If you walk with music playing, choose songs with different beats per minute then match your steps to the beat. Shorter is better.

Toes propel you forward:

Push off of the toes of your back foot, which propels you forward for your next step.

Engage your core and glutes:

Squeeze your glutes and engage your core to support your spine. Strong core muscles; the abdominal muscles, back muscles, and your butt muscles or gluteus maximus are essential to keeping your balance and walking well

Posture:

Keep your body straight and your head up. This expands

the chest cavity and increases your oxygen intake by more than 30 percent. Also, keep your eyes up ahead to help quicken your pace. Use your peripheral vision to watch where your feet will plant on the ground.

Swing your arms quickly:
An easy way to quicken your walking speed is to quicken the speed at which your arms swing back and forth. If you focus on your arms, your legs will naturally follow without the urge to lengthen your stride. Keep your arms bent and swing them back and forth in a quick and compact motion to increase momentum. Your shoulders should be relaxed and down.

During each walk, keep **STEPS** in mind. Pick a point in the distance and consciously apply the **STEPS** in reaching the point. Keep your focus on each of the 5 aspects of **STEPS**. Eventually, as your body adjusts to the quicker pace, you will just naturally move faster and with more "pep in your step"!

Begin walking! It's that simple. Go outside, and put one foot in front of the other. If you can only walk to the end of your block, great! You've made a start to a healthier you.

Tomorrow, try to walk at least 1 step further than today. Going forward you just have to keep the same mindset…"I'll walk at least 1 step further than yesterday."

You can also aim for a set amount of time. Start out walking for 5 minutes. The next day aim for 7 minutes… you get the idea.

* * *

"Being happy is a requisite for longevity."
-Chidi Prosper Agbugba

REVIEW: STEPS
- Shorter stride
- Toes propel you forward
- Engage your core and glutes
- Posture is upright
- Swing your arms quicker

Your Next Step:
How far can you walk in 10 minutes?
Test your average walking speed by doing a Time/ Distance Measurement.
- Start your watch, begin walking, then note where you have stopped after 10 minutes.
- Time yourself over the same route once per month.
- You will be pleasantly surprised each time you complete this exercise and realize you are walking faster and further!

"How do you live a long life?
Take a two-mile walk every morning before breakfast."
Harry S. Truman

July: Walking Speed: Take More STEPS to Live Longer

July 1
The secret to longevity is to keep breathing.
Sophie Tucke

July 2
Longevity is having a chronic disease and taking care of it.
Oliver Wendell Holmes

July 3
The ingredients of health and long life, are great temperance, open air, easy labor, and little care.
Philip Sidney

July 4
Longevity conquers scandal every time.
Shelby Foote

July 5
A stricken tree, a living thing, so beautiful, so dignified, so admirable in its potential longevity, is, next to man, perhaps the most touching of wounded objects.
Edna Ferber

July 6

The foods that promote longevity, virtue, strength, health, happiness, and joy; are juicy, smooth, substantial, and agreeable to the stomach.
Bhagavad Gita

July 7

The quality, not the longevity, of one's life is what is important.
Martin Luther King, Jr.

July 8

If you ask what is the single most important key to longevity, I would have to say it is avoiding worry, stress and tension. And if you didn't ask me, I'd still have to say it.
George F. Burn

July 9

A man ninety years old was asked to what he attributed his longevity. "I reckon," he said, with a twinkle in his eye, "It's because most nights I went to bed and slept when I should have sat up and worried.
Dorothea Kent

July 10

In ancient China, the Taoists taught that a constant inner smile, a smile to oneself, insured health, happiness and longevity. Why? Smiling to yourself is like basking in love: you become your own best friend. Living with an inner smile is to live in harmony with yourself.

Mantak Chia

July 11

It's never too late to get back on your feet though we won't live forever. Make sure you accomplish what you were put here for.
Abigail Adams

July 12

The various features and aspects of human life, such as longevity, good health, success, happiness, and so forth, which we consider desirable, are all dependent on kindness and a good heart.
Dalai Lama

July 13

Gratitude is a mindful awareness of the benefits of life. It's the greatest of virtues. Studies have linked the emotion with a variety of positive effects. Grateful people tend to be more empathetic and forgiving of others. People who keep a gratitude journal are more likely to have a positive outlook on life. Grateful individuals demonstrate less envy, materialism, and self-centeredness. Gratitude improves self-esteem and enhances relationships, quality of sleep, and longevity.
Max Lucado

July 14

There's no longevity, living off of negativity.
Big Pun

July 15
Mid-month Point to Ponder
Don't become a statistic
According to a study published in the Journal of the American Heart Association, and a study published in The Lancet concluded a person that exercises five times per week paid $2,500 less in annual health care expenses related to heart disease than someone who did not walk or otherwise move for 30 minutes per day five times per week!

Doctor's visits, prescriptions, lost time at work and the lost quality of life due to preventable illness all add up to a significant sum of time and money.

Look at your time and effort spent walking as an investment in yourself. What could be better than that! Your health, happiness, and life depend on it!

"We can change the expression of more than 70 percent of the genes that have a direct bearing on our health and longevity."
David Perlmutter

July 16
Those who die without being forgotten get longevity.
Laozi

July 17
THE 2000-YEAR-OLD MAN'S SECRETS OF LONGEVITY

- Don't run for a bus - there'll always be another.
- Never, ever touch fried food.
- Stay out of a Ferrari or any other small Italian car.
- Eat fruit - a nectarine - even a rotten plum is good.

Mel Brooks

July 18
Positive people have more friends which is a key factor of happiness and longevity.
Robert D. Putnam

July 19
Youth is a quality, not a matter of circumstances.
Frank Lloyd Wright

July 20
A long life may not be good enough, but a good life is long enough.
Benjamin Franklin

July 21
A sense of humor has been linked with longevity. It is a possibility that the mental attitude reflected in a lively sense of humor is an important factor predisposing some people toward long life.
Raymond Moody

July 22
The secret of long life is double careers. One to about age sixty, then another for the next thirty years.
David Ogilvy

* * *

July 23

We become what we want to be by consistently being what we want to become each day.
Richard G. Scott

July 24

There's a long life ahead of you and it's going to be beautiful, as long as you keep loving and hugging each other.
Yoko Ono

July 25

A human being would certainly not grow to be seventy or eighty years old if this longevity had no meaning for the species. The afternoon of human life must also have a significance of its own and cannot be merely a pitiful appendage to life's morning.
Carl Jung

July 26

If you want to live a long life, focus on making contributions.
Hans Selye

July 27

The secret to a long life is to stay busy, get plenty of exercise and don't drink too much. Then again, don't drink too little.
Herman Smith-Johannsen

July 28
To sustain longevity, you have to evolve.
Aries Spears

July 29
It is never too late to be who you might have been.
George Eliot

July 30
The great glorious masterpiece of man is to know how to live with purpose.
Michel de Montaigne

July 31
In the end, people will judge you anyway, so don't live our life impressing other, live your life impressing yourself.
Eunice Camacho Infante

"The young comedians always ask me, 'What's the secret for staying around?' I tell them, 'There is no secret - just stay around. Longevity is the most important thing.'"
Don Rickles

August: Transformational Process

Once you start walking, an amazing process of transformation begins to take place:

The first transformation will be physical as you will begin to feel good! It will begin slowly at first then rather quickly; your body will begin to **"feel good!"** You will "feel" your body getting into physical condition.

You won't be sore, you'll just feel like your muscles have been used. Trust me, you'll want this feeling to continue. Soon, you will find that your average walking speed has increased as you become more fit.

"Real transformation requires real honesty. If you want to move forward, get real with yourself."
- Bryant McGill

The second transformation will be your mindset. You'll begin to think more clearly, you'll be calmer, and your creativity and problem-solving skills will kick into overdrive.

Try this out; before you go out on your next walk, think of a problem you are having. For example, I open my iPhone and create a new note on my Notes app. I dictate the problem at the top of the page then... I do nothing. I just walk, enjoy my surroundings, enjoy the feeling of motion, and enjoy the sense of accomplishing something.

Then, suddenly, my mind will drift over to that problem I put down on my Notes app. When I'm walking, I find my mind just randomly goes someplace other than where I am walking, and in this state, I begin to see solutions to problems I am having.

Too often, we expend our energy on issues that have nothing to do with what we want in our lives. It's like being in a car race and constantly looking at the side mirror to see if the other car is catching up rather than focusing on what's going on in front of you.

Having a vision of what you want to achieve in life is necessary if you ever want to arrive somewhere.

The next series of quotes is about achieving success and staying focused on the goals you have set for yourself.

"Yes, your transformation will be hard. Yes, you will feel frightened, messed up and knocked down. Yes, you'll want to stop. Yes, it's the best work you'll ever do."
*- **Robin Sharma***

Your Next Step

Get out and begin walking today! I can't explain it other than when I'm out walking I see the problem differently and the solutions come quickly. As if through some mystical process, most times the solution comes to me near the very end of my walk!

Walking for Health and Fitness: is a health, fitness, and wellness website dedicated to walking
and all the physical, psychological, and spiritual benefits that comes from it in order to achieve a healthy, balanced lifestyle!
Visit at: www.walkingforhealthandfitness.com/

August: Transformational Process

August 1
Nothing gets transformed in your life until your mind is transformed.
Ifeanyi Enoch Onuoha

August 2
When you look at the sun during your walking meditation, the mindfulness of the body helps you to see that the sun is in you; without the sun there is no life at all and suddenly you get in touch with the sun in a different way.
Thich Nhat Hanh

August 3
Things work out best for those who make the best of how things work out.
John Wooden

August 4
As the caterpillar undergoes transformation within the cocoon before emerging as a butterfly; likewise, life experiences shape character.
Lorna Jackie

August 5
Change can be hard. It requires no extra effort to settle for the same old thing. Auto-pilot keeps us locked into past patterns. But transforming your life? That requires

courage, commitment, and effort. It's tempting to stay camped in the zone of That's-Just-How-It-Is. But to get to the really good stuff in life, you have to be willing to become an explorer and adventurer.
John Mark Green

August 6
Transformation is an ongoing process that tends to appear ordinary, when, in fact, something extraordinary is taking place.
Suzy Ross

August 7
It's the not exactly knowing of the way, the map thrown away that makes the setting sun the guide, and makes the setting come alive.
Art Garfunkel

August 8
First comes thought; then organization of that thought, into ideas and plans; then transformation of those plans into reality. The beginning, as you will observe, is in your imagination.
Napoleon Hill

August 9
Real transformation requires real honesty. If you want to move forward – get real with yourself.
Bryant McGill

August 10
Change is inevitable, but transformation is by conscious choice.

Heather Ash Amara

August 11
Transformation isn't sweet and bright. It's a dark and murky, painful pushing. An unraveling of the untruths you've carried in your body. A practice in facing your own created demons. A complete uprooting, before becoming.
Victoria Erickson

August 12
You're always one decision away from a totally different life.
Anonymous

August 13
You and I possess within ourselves at every moment of our lives, under all circumstances, the power to transform the quality of our lives.
Werner Erhard

August 14
It's not about perfect. It's about effort. And when you implement that effort into your life. Every single day, that's where transformation happens. That's how change occurs. Keep going. Remember why you started.
Anonymous

August 15
Mid-month Point to Ponder:
Here is a reminder that in January, I asked: "where will you be one year from now?"

* * *

The question in August is the same: Where will you be one year from now?

- Do you have an answer?
- Are you still searching for your "why?"
- Are you on the right path?

Every day is a new opportunity to begin anew.

The first quote in this book's introduction is: "A year from now you'll wish you started today." I hope you do!

"Nothing happens until the pain of remaining the same outweighs the pain of change."
Arthur Burt

"If every day you practice walking and sitting meditation and generate the energy of mindfulness and concentration and peace, you are a cell in the body of the new Buddha. This is not a dream but is possible today and tomorrow."
Thich Nhat Hanh

August 16
You're transforming old patterns of your mind and letting go of thoughts you don't need to have around any longer.
Anonymous

August 17
The key to our transformation is simply this: the better we know ourselves the better equipped we will be to make

our choices wisely.
Gregg Braden

August 18
When someone chooses to value herself over the things she can buy, true transformation begins.
Suze Orman

August 19
May the next few months be a period of magnificent transformation.
Anonymous

August 20
Transformation does not start with someone else changing you; transformation is an inner self reworking of what you are now to what you will be.
Byron Pulsifer

August 21
Don't fear failure. Fear being in the exact same place next year as you are today.
Michael Hyatt

August 22
We need to realize that our path to transformation is through our mistakes. We're meant to make mistakes, recognize them, and move on to become unlimited.
Yehuda Berg

August 23
If you want to be great and successful, choose people who

are great and successful and walk side by side with them.
Ralph Waldo Emerson

August 24
Embrace each challenge in your life as an opportunity for self-transformation.
Bernie S. Siegel

August 25
I know this transformation is painful, but you're not falling into something different, with a new capacity to be beautiful.
William C. Hannan

August 26
I've never seen any life transformation that didn't begin with the person in question finally getting tired of their own nonsense.
Elizabeth Gilbert

August 27
You have to love yourself enough to set a standard for your life that you're unwilling to compromise. If you accept the standards of others for your life you'll never be happy.
Tony Gaskins

August 28
Personal transformation can and does have global effects. As we go, so goes the world, for the world is us. The revolution that will save the world is ultimately a personal one.
Marianne Williamson

* * *

August 29
Transformation literally means going beyond your form.
Wayne Dyer

August 30
If you start thinking of stress as not a bad thing but inevitable, resulting in change that itself leads to transformation that leads to sharp and radical changes… it can be a very useful way of thinking.
Marilyn Ferguson

August 31
Transformation in the world happens when people are healed and start investing in other people.
Michael W. Smith

"Intelligence is the ability to adapt to change."
Stephen Hawking

September: Developing a Positive Mindset

The Power of Affirmations - Why Affirmations Work

You're awesome! But sometimes life has a way of causing you to forget this. Work, family commitments, and all the running around we do each day; sometimes you get taken for granted. Not here, and not by me.

So, let me repeat, You're Awesome! But you don't need me telling you that, you need to tell yourself that.

"Once you replace negative thoughts with positive ones,
you'll start having positive results."
— Willie Nelson

Exercise and Affirmations

Developing a positive mindset is one of the most powerful and transformative habits you can include in your daily routine. Listening to affirmations while you are walking will supercharge the effects of the affirmations.

Physical activity stresses our brain in the same way that it stresses our muscles. Like active muscle fibers, neurons of the brain break down then recover to become stronger and more resilient with exercise.

* * *

It's an essential part of your overall health and well-being, and one that we will work on together to transform your life and fill you with new passion, energy, and joy!

Developing a Positive Mindset is an Important Element of Your Life Success

Affirmations are simply positive statements that describe a desired situation. "I am healthy, happy, and radiant!" is an example. It's a positive statement that describes your desire to be a healthy, happy, and radiant person.

Positive affirmations help your internal dialog to create a new vision you have of yourself and your life. Affirmations are repeated several times so the subconscious mind can spring into action.

Repetition is the key to reinforcing the learning and embedding the new thoughts into your mind.

Accomplished people from all walks of life use affirmations along with other powerful positive thinking techniques to help them achieve their goals. The mind and its thoughts are a powerful force that, when used positively, can help you achieve whatever you set out to accomplish.

Your subconscious mind accepts as true whatever you say to yourself. Whether you think you can do something or not, you are correct!

The words you tell yourself work to create or destroy your dreams. Many times, we're not even fully aware of the words and statements that play in our minds or the impact they're having on what we wish to create.

Your subconscious mind accepts as true whatever you say to yourself.

"Positive thinking will let you do everything better than negative thinking will."
-Zig Ziglar

Positive Affirmations Work to Program Your Mind:
- Affirmations keep your mind focused and influence and activate the power of your subconscious mind.
- Affirmations are positive statements that help you change the way you think and act.
- Affirmations make you feel more positive and energized. They help you to reflect on your true nature.

You can use positive affirmations to your advantage due to the repetition which helps focus your mind and creates corresponding thoughts or images in your mind.

Your subconscious mind accepts the thought or image as being true and will continue to nurture and grow this thought.

Listening to positive affirmations consciously and intently will help you to transform your habits, your behaviors, your attitude and have a dramatic effect on your quality of life.

* * *

In my my Mindful Walking Exercise Program, the 30-minute audio track; Mindful Walking Exercise Session-1 was designed to get you moving with its upbeat music, then to focus your mind on the positive affirmations spoken over the music.

The combination of positive statements and reminders to breathe as you walk will turn the 30-minute walk into a calming, almost meditative experience. You will feel refreshed and ready to face any challenge that comes your way.

Results from listening to the affirmations will vary depending on several factors such as the amount of time, focus, faith, and energy you invest in listening to the audio track.

Focus on the positive feeling you get while walking and listening. You will soon begin to notice a shift in your energy levels and experience generally good feelings.

Improve Your Mind-Body Connection
You have an extraordinary mind. As the poet John Milton writes in Paradise Lost, "The mind is its own place, and in itself can make a heaven of hell and a hell of heaven."

The act of walking makes you more productive. Exercise improves cognition in two ways:

- Exercise increases oxygen flow into the brain.
- Exercise reduces brain-bound free radicals.

* * *

One of the most interesting findings of the past few decades is that an increase in oxygen is always accompanied by an uptick in mental sharpness. Exercise acts directly on the molecular machinery of the brain itself. It increases neurons' creation, survival, and resistance to damage and stress.

Walking Meditation

Walking, combined with mindful breathing, is by far the most practical and easy to implement method of walking meditation. It has the added benefit of providing exercise for mind and body at the same time!

- Begin by moving slowly, to find a rhythm to your movements and breathing.
- After you hit that sweet spot where movement and breath get into sync, you can move at any pace you want and walk as long as you like.
- Practice the 4-3 Breathing pattern.
- Inhale for 4 steps, exhale for 3 steps.

The goal is not to make it an effort, but to make it effortless and mindless… meaning that your mind is focused only on the activity itself and not the rest of your day, your problems, your work, or your to-do list.

The goal is to be fully present in the activity of rhythmic movement and breathing.

Your Next Step:

We are so often faced with negativity—negative news, negative perspectives—from pessimistic people that it becomes difficult to continue keeping a positive spirit.

Instead of getting dragged down in the negativity of others, turn to optimistic people who have figured out how to see the brighter side of life and remain positive no matter what… so you can learn to do the same.

Learn more about the **Mindful Walking Exercise Program** from Walking for Health and Fitness.

You will be transformed as the messages remind you of just how special you are.

"We can complain because rose bushes have thorns, or rejoice because thorn bushes have roses."
Abraham Lincoln

September: Developing a Positive Mindset

September 1
Surround yourself with the dreamers, and the doers, the believers, and thinkers, but most of all, surround yourself with those who see the greatness within you, even when you don't see it yourself.
Edmund Lee

September 2
In order to carry a positive action we must develop here a positive vision.
Dalai Lama

September 3
Be the attitude you want to be around.
Tim DeTellis

September 4
When you want to succeed as much as you want to breathe, that's when you will be successful.
Author Unknown

September 5
You'll never really see how toxic someone is until you breathe fresher air.

Author Unknown

September 6
Keep your face to the sunshine and you cannot see a shadow.
Helen Keller

September 7
Yesterday is not ours to recover, but tomorrow is ours to win or lose.
Lyndon B. Johnson

September 8
Happiness is a quality of the soul…not a function of one's material circumstances.
Aristotle

September 9
Positive thinking will let you do everything better than negative thinking will.
Zig Ziglar

September 10
Pessimism leads to weakness, optimism to power.
William James

September 11
You can't make positive choices for the rest of your life without an environment that makes those choices easy, natural, and enjoyable.
Deepak Chopra

* * *

September 12

The thing that lies at the foundation of positive change, the way I see it, is service to a fellow human being.
Lee Iacocca

September 13

Positive thinking is more than just a tagline. It changes the way we behave. And I firmly believe that when I am positive, it not only makes me better, but it also makes those around me better.
Harvey Mackay

September 14

In every day, there are 1,440 minutes. That means we have 1,440 daily opportunities to make a positive impact.
Les Brown

September 15

Mid-month Point to Ponder

Have you been dragged down by:
- Doctor's visits
- High costs of prescription drugs
- Lost time at work
- A lessened quality of life due to preventable illness

These all add up to a significant sum of time and money.

That was me until I slowed down, got smarter about what exercise was all about, and harness the power of my mindset to get back into shape... and stay in shape!

THERE IS A BETTER WAY:

- WALK for 30-minutes
- LISTEN to music and positive affirmations
- CONNECT your mind and body

YOU'RE AWESOME!
But sometimes life has a way of causing you to forget this. Work, family commitments, and all the running around we do each day; sometimes you get taken for granted. Not here and not by me.

EXERCISE AND AFFIRMATIONS
Developing a positive mindset is one of the most powerful and transformative habits you can include in your daily routine. Listening to affirmations while you are walking will supercharge the effects of the affirmations.

"I'm a very positive thinker, and I think that is what helps me the most in difficult moments."
Roger Federer

"Perpetual optimism is a force multiplier."
Colin Powell

"You are the average of the five people you spend the most time with."
Jim Rohn

September 16
Attitude is a little thing that makes a big difference.
Winston Churchill

* * *

September 17

Let us rise up and be thankful, for if we didn't learn a lot today, at least we learned a little, and if we didn't learn a little, at least we didn't get sick, and if we got sick, at least we didn't die; so let us all be thankful.
Buddha

September 18

You can, you should, and if you're brave enough to start, you will.
Stephen King

September 19

What is the difference between an obstacle and an opportunity? Our attitude toward it. Every opportunity has a difficult, and every difficulty has an opportunity.
J. Sidlow Baxter

September 20

Good thoughts and actions can never produce bad results; bad thoughts and actions can never produce good results...We understand this law in the natural world, and work with it; but few understand it in the mental and moral world – although its operation there is just as simple and undeviating – and they, therefore, do not cooperate with it.
James Allen

September 21

Life is a gift, and it offers us the privilege, opportunity and responsibility to give something back by becoming more.
Tony Robbins

* * *

September 22
Don't be pushed around by the fears in your mind. Be led by the dreams in your heart.
Roy T. Bennett

September 23
The only place where your dreams become impossible is in your own thinking.
Robert H. Shuller

September 24
Cultivate an optimistic mind, use your imagination, always consider alternatives, and dare to believe that you can make possible what others think is impossible.
Rodolfo Costa

September 25
Beliefs that are good promote your potential and enhance your unique special qualities.
Deborah Day

September 26
When you are joyful, when you say yes to life and have fun and project positivity all around you, you become a sun in the center of every constellation, and people want to be near you.
Shannon L. Alder

September 27
The most important thing you will ever wear is your attitude.

Jeff Moore

September 28
It's a funny thing about life, once you begin to take note of the things you are grateful for, you begin to lose sight of the things that you lack.
Germany Kent

September 29
The greatest discovery of all time is that a person can change his future by merely changing his attitude.
Oprah Winfrey

September 30
An attitude of positive expectation is the mark of the superior personality.
Brian Tracy

"Optimism is the most important human trait, because it allows us to evolve our ideas, to improve our situation, and to hope for a better tomorrow."
Seth Godin

October: Staying Motivated

Let's face it, life sometimes gets in the way of our hope, dreams, goals, and plans. Have you ever thought of giving up on your goals when the challenges you face seem to big to overcome?

I have. And so have many others.

"That which does not kill us makes us stronger."
-Friedrich Nietzsche

Our commitment to those goals and dreams are tested often. When roadblocks appear, it seems so easy to turn back.

The good news is that when you overcome these challenges and stay committed to your dreams, fantastic things happen! You build character and discover what you are made of. It brings out your most authentic self.

What is Motivation?
The definition of motivation is the reason you have for acting or behaving in a particular way.

You need to find that one thing to inspire you to walk. Here are several suggestions to help keep you moving. Of course, your reason for walking may not be on this list and that's just great as long as you have a reason, any reason to keep moving!

- Soak up the sunshine
- Aches and pains can't catch you
- 1,000 extra steps a day help you lose weight
- Tracking your steps and mileage is exciting
- Changing your walking routes changes your calorie burn
- Walking every day is powerful medicine: Walking improves brain function, immune function, bone health, breast health, mood, and heart health
- 15-minutes a day = more energy
- Easy to tone while on the road – add one or more of the following bodyweight fitness movements and you add metabolism-boosting power to your next walk. Pushups, lunges, squats, and planks
- A deeper connection to others
- Develop greater confidence

Have a Goal

It's worth repeating from my February lesson that goals give us a purpose! Here is a review of the seven steps that will help you to set and achieve your goals!

- Decide exactly what you want in terms of health and fitness
- Write down your goals and make them measurable
- Set a deadline
- Identify all the obstacles that you will have to overcome to achieve your goals
- Determine the additional knowledge and skills that you will require to achieve your goals
- Determine those people whose help and

cooperation you will require to achieve your goals

- Make a list of all your answers to the above, and organize them by sequence and priority

By following these seven steps, you can accomplish any goal that you set for yourself.

If you have not set your goal yet, then reread the above steps and get started on the road to successful walking!

"Goals allow you to control the direction of change in your favor"
- Brian Tracy

Write It Down

Add as much information as you need to "paint" a complete picture of your walking health and fitness routine. I'm constantly added elements to my mileage worksheet and adjusting my goals.

Sign up for more information about *The Walking for Health and Fitness Complete Program.* Included in the program is the Walking and *Fitness Daily Journal.*

Fill in your information each day to monitor your progress. It's a great feeling when you look back 6-months from now and see, **in writing,** how far you've come as a walker.

The Journal will keep you honest. Having a blank entry will get you moving.

10 Ways to Stay Motivated:
- **Create a Vision Board:** This will help you visualize your intended results and allow you to see your ideal future! As you create the vision board, your creativity will begin to shine through and fire up your imagination as you create your future
- **Break your goals down into smaller pieces:** "Chunk it down"
- **Treat yourself** whenever you have achieved these smaller pieces
- **Share your walking goals** with supportive people
- **Keep yourself organized** by having a walking routine
- **Keep the big picture in mind**
- **Don't worry** about what you can't control
- **Seek out positive information**
- **Remind yourself** why you set your goals
- **Be consistent**

"Believe in yourself! Have faith in your abilities! Without a humble but reasonable confidence in your own powers, you cannot be successful or happy."
- Norman Vincent Peale

Your Next Step:
Set or adjust your goals, then incorporate some or all of the 10 ways to stay motivated into your walking routine.

Watch my YouTube video series: <u>Keys to Staying</u> <u>Motivated</u>

"Breathe in inspiration and trust yourself that the answer is yes you can."
- Author Unknown

October: Staying Motivated

October 1
Start where you are. Use what you have. Do what you can.
Arthur Ashe

October 2
If you are not willing to risk the usual you will have to
settle for the ordinary.
Jim Rohn

October 3
Believe in yourself! Have faith in your abilities! Without a
humble but reasonable confidence in your own powers
you cannot be successful or happy.
Norman Vincent Peale

October 4
If you can dream it, you can do it.
Walt Disney

October 5
Do not wait; the time will never be 'just right.' Start where
you stand, and work with whatever tools you may have at
your command, and better tools will be found as you go
along.
George Herbert

October 6

The future belongs to those who believe in the beauty of their dreams.

Eleanor Roosevelt

October 7

Aim for the moon. If you miss, you may hit a star.

W. Clement Stone

October 8

There are two types of people who will tell you that you cannot make a difference in this world: those who are afraid to try and those who are afraid you will succeed.

Ray Goforth

October 9

Courage is resistance to fear, mastery of fear--not absence of fear

Mark Twain

October 10

There will be obstacles. There will be doubters. There will be mistakes. But with hard work, there are no limits.

Michael Phelps

October 11

We aim above the mark to hit the mark.

Ralph Waldo Emerson

October 12

Change your life today. Don't gamble on the future, act now, without delay.
Simone de Beauvoir

October 13

You just can't beat the person who never gives up.
Babe Ruth

October 14

Why should you continue going after your dreams? Because seeing the look on the faces of the people who said you couldn't... will be priceless.
Kevin Ngo

October 15

Mid-month Point to Ponder

The definition of motivation is the "reason you have for acting or behaving in a particular way."

You need to find that one thing to inspire you to walk. If you haven't done so yet, go back over the list of 10 Ways to Stay Motivated from this month's introduction and pick one to work on.

My suggestion is to create your Vision Board, here's why:
- Vision boards provide a daily reminder of what you really want
- Vision boards help you get unstuck
- Vision boards fire up your emotions

What to put on your Vision Board:
- Images of what you would like to have come into your life
- Motivation quotes (download the quote images from this books resource page)
- Pictures of the most important people in your life.

Put your Vision Board up in a place where you can look at it every day. Mine is located next to my work desk. Look at it often throughout the day.

A key component to using a Vision Board is the **emotional aspect** of it. You must have an emotional reaction when looking at the board. Look at one of the images and **imagine how you will feel** by having it come into your life.

Your emotional connection to the Vision board will bring you success!

By continuing to link the image to your feelings, you speed up the process of having it come into your life!

"If you don't design your own life plan, chances are you'll fall into someone else's plan. And guess what they have planned for you? Not much."
- Jim Rohn

"Where there is a will, there is a way. If there is a chance in a million that you can do something, anything, to keep what you want from ending, do it. Pry the door open or, if need be, wedge your foot in that door and keep it open."
- Pauline Kael

"Just when the caterpillar thought the world was ending, he turned into a butterfly."
- Proverb

October 16
In my experience, there is only one motivation, and that is desire. No reasons or principle contain it or stand against it.
Jane Smiley

October 17
Understanding motivation is one of the most important things we can do in our lives, because it has such a bearing on why we do the things we do and whether we enjoy them or not.
Clayton Christensen

October 18
The best motivation is self-motivation. The guy says, 'I wish someone would come by and turn me on.' What if they don't show up? You've got to have a better plan for your life.
Jim Rohn

* * *

October 19
The success of our efforts depends not so much on the efforts themselves, but rather on our motive for doing them.
Denis Waitley

October 20
The difference between a successful person and others is not a lack of strength, not a lack of knowledge, but rather in a lack of will.
Vince Lombardi

October 21
People often say that motivation doesn't last. Well, neither does bathing—that's why we recommend it daily.
Zig Ziglar

October 22
You can motivate by fear, and you can motivate by reward. But both those methods are only temporary. The only lasting thing is self-motivation.
Homer Rice

October 23
Be miserable. Or motivate yourself. Whatever has to be done, it's always your choice.
Wayne Dyer

October 24
Take up one idea. Make that one idea your life--think of it, dream of it, live on that idea. Let the brain, muscles,

nerves, every part of your body, be full of that idea, and just leave every other idea alone. This is the way to success.
Swami Vivekananda

October 25
Good things come to people who wait, but better things come to those who go out and get them.
Anonymous

October 26
A successful man is one who can lay a firm foundation with the bricks others have thrown at him.
David Brinkley

October 27
The whole secret of a successful life is to find out what is one's destiny to do, and then do it.
Henry Ford

October 28
What seems to us as bitter trials are often blessings in disguise.
Oscar Wilde

October 29
Too many of us are not living our dreams because we are living our fears.
Les Brown

October 30
People who succeed have momentum. The more they succeed, the more they want to succeed, and the more they

find a way to succeed. Similarly, when someone is failing, the tendency is to get on a downward spiral that can even become a self-fulfilling prophecy.
Tony Robbins

October 31
Life is not about finding yourself. Life is about creating yourself.
Lolly Daskal

"If you want to make a permanent change, stop focusing on the size of your problems and start focusing on the size of you!"
T. Harv Eker

November: The Power of Your Brain

Exercise affects more than just your muscles. When you walk and do bodyweight exercises you are increasing your heart rate which pumps more oxygen to the brain.

- Exercise releases hormones that provide an excellent environment for the growth of brain cells.
- Exercise stimulates the growth of new connections between cells in many important cortical areas of the brain.
- Exercise has a positive effect on the brain's ability to change. This is commonly referred to as brain plasticity.
- Exercise increases the growth factors in the brain which makes it easier for the brain to grow new neuronal connections.

The more you challenge your body, the more you focus your brain.

"The mind is a powerful force. It can enslave us or empower us. It can plunge us into the depths of misery or take us to the heights of ecstasy. Learn to use the power wisely."
- David Cuschieri

Human Evolution

Humans evolved to move; the acts of hunting, running, foraging, and climbing all involved movement and encouraged brain growth that eventually separated us from other animals.

Physical activity stresses our brain in the same way that it stresses our muscles. Like active muscle fibers, neurons of the brain break down then recover to become stronger and more resilient with exercise.

Protects Our Most Important Organ

Physical activity prompts the brain to create enzymes that "eat up" any existing amyloid beta-protein plaque that overpowers and strangles healthy neurons. This plaque has been implicated as the cause of dementia symptoms and a contributing factor to Alzheimer's Disease.

Physical activity boost executive function (collection of abilities that help us plan ahead, reason, and solve complex problems). Exercise slows the natural decline in executive function and aerobic exercise at a younger age can protect against this decline later in life.

Complex movement results in complex brain growth. Exercising as little as 30-minutes per day, 3 times per week improves executive function and brain performance!

"When you become the master of your mind, you are master of everything."

- Swami Satchidananda

Boost Memory Retention & Learning Capacity

Exercise increases the size of the hippocampus which is involved in the formation of new memories and associated with learning and emotion. The brain literally grows each time you exercise

Studies have shown just walking 30-35 minutes increases cognitive flexibility which allows us to shift thinking and switch between topics. Physical activity leads to brain plasticity; the ability of our brain to grow and change.

Improved Movement & Coordination

Exercise stimulates the cerebellum, the part of the brain that works to coordinate the body. The cerebellum is also linked to the prefrontal cortex where judgment and decision-making occur.

Intensifies Creativity & Imagination

Exercise "lights up" the hippocampus during exercise which stimulates the imagination and encourages thoughts of future plans. The hippocampus is the root of creative and inspirational thinking.

Steve Jobs, and many other creative types relied on walking to enhance their imaginations. Jobs' walking meetings became part of his workday. In a recent study, a person walking - whether on a treadmill facing a blank wall or walking outside in fresh air produced twice as many creative responses compared to a person sitting down.

* * *

Encourages Mood Stability
Scientists have encouraged exercise as a treatment for depression and anxiety-related disorders for years. Studies of daily yoga and meditation have shown shrinkage of the amygdala, a deep-brain structure strongly linked to the processing of stress, fear, and anxiety.
A smaller amygdala means a lower rate of concern and worry and a heightened sense of calm allowing us to concentrate on the task at hand.

Exercise has been shown to be as effective as antidepressants for patients with major depressive disorders. The increase in serotonin production (happy mood neurotransmitters) during exercise is responsible for the alleviation of chronic depression. Exercise helps normalize sleep which is known to be protective of the brain.

Increase Alertness & Perception
The brain contains 100 billion neurons which talk to each other to govern our every thought and action. Neurons talk to each other more efficiently when we are exercising. Physical activity turns on the switch that controls arousal and attention.

Neurotransmitter synthesis is boosted by exercise:
- Norepinephrine: focus, motivation, and determination
- Serotonin: mood, impulsivity, and aggression.
- Dopamine: controls our sense of contentment and reward.

* * *

They all improve cognition and healthy ambition.

The brain becomes more receptive to incoming information during exercise. The more you challenge your body, the more you focus your brain.

Your Next Step
Make a plan for your next several 30-minute walks.
- Write down where you'll do them.
- Check G-map pedometer, or other similar web-based sites, to map out your walking route and distance.
- You'll find the link on the *Walking Inspiration* **resource page.**

"The human brain has 100 billion neurons, each neuron connected to 10 thousand other neurons. Sitting on your shoulders is the most complicated object in the known universe."
Michio Kaku

November: The Power of Your Brain

November 1
Physical fitness is not only one of the most important keys to a healthy body, it is the basis of dynamic and creative intellectual activity.
John F. Kennedy

November 2
To keep the body in good health is a duty...otherwise we shall not be able to keep our mind strong and clear.
Buddha

November 3
Exercise is like an addiction. Once you're in it, you feel like your body needs it.
Elsa Pataky

November 4
Physical activity is an excellent stress-buster and provides other health benefits as well. It also can improve your mood and self image.
Jon Wickham

November 5
Exercise and temperance can preserve something of our early strength even in old age.
Cicero

* * *

November 6
Nothing lifts me out of a bad mood better than a hard work out on my treadmill. It never fails. Exercise is nothing short of a miracle.
Cher

November 7
Research says getting regular exercise is one of the most effective ways to cope with stress.
Chris Meno

November 8
I feel better in my mind when I work out. It makes everything better.
Keri Russell

November 9
To enjoy the glow of good health, you must exercise.
Gene Tunney

November 10
Exercise to stimulate, not to annihilate. The world wasn't formed in a day, and neither were we. Set small goals and build upon them.
Lee Haney

November 11
Training gives us an outlet for suppressed energies created by stress and thus tones the spirit just as exercise conditions the body.
Arnold Schwarzenegger

* * *

November 12

Few people know how to take a walk. The qualifications are endurance, plain clothes, old shoes, an eye for nature, good humor, vast curiosity, good speech, good silence and nothing too much.
Ralph Waldo Emerson

November 13

If we could give every individual the right amount of nourishment and exercise, not too little and not too much, we would have found the safest way to health.
Hippocrates

November 14

Every thought we think is creating our future.
Louise Hay

November 15

Mid-month Point to Ponder

Your brain has the ability to send and receive an enormous amount of information. Doctors and scientists don't yet completely understand the full complexity of the brain.

Here are some facts about your brain:
- An adult brain weighs about 3 pounds.
- About 75 percent of the brain is made up of water. This means that dehydration, even in small amounts, can have a negative effect on the brain functions.
- Headaches are caused by a chemical reaction in your brain combined with the muscles and nerves of your neck and head.

- Information runs between neurons in your brain for everything we see, think, or do. These neurons move information at different speeds. The fastest speed for information to pass between neurons is about 250 mph.
- Dreams are believed to be a combination of imagination, psychological factors, and neurological factors. They prove that your brain is working even when you are sleeping.
- Your brain uses 20 percent of the oxygen and blood in your body.

Using your Brain Power:
You are just a few steps away from solving your most pressing problems. How to problem-solve while walking will give you the tools to take action on your most pressing concerns.

"Movement is a medicine for creating change in a person's physical, emotional, and mental states."
- Carol Welch

"It is a shame for a man to grow old without seeing the beauty and strength of which his body is capable."
- Socrates

"Exercise and application produce order in our affairs,
health of body, cheerfulness of mind,
and these make us precious to our friends."
- Thomas Jefferson

November 16
True enjoyment comes from activity of the mind and
exercise of the body; the two are ever united.
Wilhelm Von Humboldt

November 17
We do not stop exercising because we grow old - we grow
old because we stop exercising.
Kenneth Cooper

November 18
Whatever we plant in our subconscious mind and nourish
with repetition and emotion will one day become a reality.
Earl Nightingale

November 19
You have power over your mind – not outside events.
Realize this, and you will find strength.
Marcus Aurelius

November 20
The mind is a powerful force. It can enslave us or empower
us. It can plunge us into the depths of misery or take us to
the heights of ecstasy. Learn to use the power wisely.
David Cuschieri

* * *

November 21
Your mind is your greatest power. use it well.
Aneta Cruz

November 22
The mind is everything. What you think you become.
Buddha

November 23
If you realized how powerful your thoughts are, you would never think a negative thought.
Anonymous

November 24
Your mind is a powerful thing. When you fill it with positive thoughts, your life will start to change.
Anonymous

November 25
Our life is the creation of our mind.
Buddha

November 26
We are what we believe we are.
Anonymous

November 27
Whatever you hold in your mind will tend to occur in your life.
Anonymous

* * *

November 28
Your mind is precious. It has the power to unlock infinite possibilities.
Joel Annesley

November 29
There is no limit to the power of the human mind. The more concentrated it is, the more power is brought to bear on one point.
Swami Vivekananda

November 30
Focused mind power is one of the strongest forces on earth.
Mark Victor Hansen

"The mind is its own place and in itself, can make a Heaven of Hell,
a Hell of Heaven."
John Milton

December: Establishing Morning and Walking Exercise Routines

Why Have a Morning Routine

A morning routine sets the tone for your day. Having this daily ritual in place will help you overcome procrastination. You wake up, begin performing the first activity of the morning and you've started your day off on the right foot by taking action!

Developing Your Morning Routine

I suggest beginning with 2 or 3 activities to get you into the groove. Perform each activity for 5 to 10 minutes.

Suggestions:
- Read
- Write
- Exercise
- Stretch
- Meditate
- Family time
- Listen to music, podcasts, or audiobooks
- Be creative by painting, sketching, or coloring
- Recite affirmations to supercharge your mindset

As you become accustomed to starting your day with your daily routine, these new habits will evolve to give you exactly what you need to be the best version of you!

* * *

"Lose an hour in the morning, and you will spend all day looking for it."
Richard Whately

Having a "Get Out the Door" Routine
Many athletes, even professionals, say that the hardest part of training is just getting out the door and starting their work-out!

Being organized is beneficial to any fitness routine. The less you have to think about, the more you can focus on the workout ahead.

Walking is an easy sport to prepare for, and **having a checklist** will save you time and effort as you prepare for your walk!

Over time, getting out the door will be automatic, but a reminder of what to bring along with you is always helpful!

"Repetition and routine allow our imagination to flourish."
- Haruki Murakami, Writer

Your Next Step:
- Develop a routine for getting out the door.
- Follow the suggestions in the **Get Out the Door Checklist on the resource page.**
- Warm-up
- Walk and do bodyweight fitness exercises.

- Incorporate strength training into your routine
- Cool-down
- Stretch
- Improve your eating habits
- Drink more water
- Get more sleep
- Breathe Deeply
- Enjoy the process of Walking for Health and Fitness!

*"Give me six hours to chop down a tree
and I will spend the first four sharpening the axe."*
- Abraham Lincoln

Your Last Step:
If you have not done so yet, go to the **Walking Inspiration resource page** and get your copy of the Walking for Health and Fitness "Get Out the Door" Checklist.

*"If you had half an hour of exercise this morning,
you're in the right frame of mind to sit still and focus
on this paragraph, and your brain is far more equipped
to remember it."*
John J. Ratey and Eric Hagerman

December: Establishing a Routine

December 1
For the past thirty-three years, I have looked in the mirror every morning and asked myself: 'If today were the last day of my life, would I want to do what I am about to do today?' And whenever the answer has been 'No' for too many days in a row, I know I need to change something.
Steve Jobs

December 2
Successful people aren't born that way. They become successful by establishing the habit of doing things unsuccessful people don't like to do. The successful people don't always like doing these things themselves; they just get on and do them.
Don Marquis

December 3
Think in the morning. Act in the noon. Eat in the evening. Sleep in the night.
William Blake

December 4
Your current life is the result of your previous choices, if you want something different, begin to choose differently.
Joe Tichio

December 5

I put my phone as far across the room as possible the night before to force me out of bed when the alarm goes off.
Josh Gross

December 6

I don't recommend my routine, but I do recommend evaluating your routine and developing one that supports the things you love the most.
George Foreman III

December 7

My routine is there to serve as the building blocks for a successful day. It's a tool. I try not to get bogged down if I can't do it all.
Carly Stein

December 8

We change our behavior when the pain of staying the same becomes greater than the pain of changing. Consequences give us the pain that motivates us to change.
Henry Cloud

December 9

Having a routine is great, but only if it serves your goals. If it's not doing that, it's called a rut.
Josh LaJaunie

December 10
Efficiency is doing things right; effectiveness is doing the right things.
Peter Drucker

December 11
Waking up early, connecting with nature, and having my quiet time are priorities to me, and they are non-negotiable.
Danette May

December 12
Starting my day with exercise gives me a big mood and energy boost throughout the day and makes me feel like I've accomplished something right off the bat.
Jake Knapp

December 13
Routines are powerful when they become rituals that no longer require conscious thought and willpower. Without iteration, however, they can become stale and can be hard to keep up.
Joel Gascoigne

December 14
When I set out my workout clothes the night before, I usually go. When I don't, I usually don't. It's amazing how much of a difference mentally that one step makes for me the next day.
Christy Wright

December 15

Mid-month Point to Ponder

Continue with your morning routine! Add and adjust activities as you see fit. Most of all, enjoy your morning time!

My Morning Routine:

- Wake up at 5 am then immediately start brewing my coffee
- I perform a series of movements and stretches for my back. This usually takes 5-minutes
- Pour my coffee
- Sit at my computer and read from a list of affirmations I've put together to fire up my mindset
- Write one quote into my daily planner (5 min. research and write)
- Read for 10 minutes
- Write in a journal for at least 10 minutes

This routine sets me up for a productive day. I've already taken care of my back, fed my brain with affirmations, fed my soul with coffee, added to my quote book, read about my current interests, and did some writing. All before my morning shower! This is what I call a good start for the day!

"It's been said that the first hour is the rudder of the day. I've found this to be very true in my own life. If I'm lazy or haphazard in my actions during the first hour after I wake up, I tend to have a fairly lazy and unfocused day."
Steve Pavlina

"It feels like I'm on the back foot if I don't complete my routine. I actually feel as though I've robbed myself of a nurturing, positivity laden start to the day."
Rochelle Livingstone

"Watch your thoughts; they become words. Watch your words; they become actions. Watch your actions; they become habit. Watch your habits; they become character. Watch your character; it becomes your destiny."
Lao Tzu

December 16
When I find something I value, I systematize it into my daily habits. Then I live by my values freely and effortlessly.
Joshua Spodek

December 17
When I follow my routine, I feel on top of the world. Regardless of what the day has in store for me, I feel accomplished and in control.

Todd Davis

December 18
Routines are the ideal way to bookend your day. I think they are the building blocks of effectiveness, efficiency, and efficacy.
Mike Vardy

December 19
I think routines should flex and change. Mine feels like a dynamic, malleable thing that emerges organically, rather than a ridgid set of steps I have to follow or plan for.
Kate Nafisi

December 20
As I've gotten older, time feels like an increasingly rare commodity, so I try to be more mindful of how I use it.
Liz Fosslien

December 21
Good habits are worth being fanatical about.
John Irving

December 22
The most important thing I do each morning is steady myself by not allowing a sense of urgency to penetrate.
Matthew Weatherley-White

December 23
I can't stress enough how important it is to wake up and go to bed at the same time on weekdays and weekends.
Bedros Keuilian

* * *

December 24
There is enormous power in nailing your morning routine, but there's even more power in adapting to it when it doesn't happen as we'd like.
Terri Schneider

December 25
The silence in the morning holds lots of expectations and is more hopeful than the silence at night.
Victoria Durnak

December 26
Every morning we are born again. What we do today is what matters most.
Buddha

December 27
Eating right and taking the time to slow down and plan in the morning is crucial to a productive day.
David Moore

December 28
Giving myself time, care, and attention in the morning has been crucial to significantly reducing my stress levels and consistently increasing my capacity to perform, have clarity, and take action.
Aiste Gazdar

December 29
I need at least a few minutes of solitude, I need a healthy breakfast, and I need to feel like I'm prepared for the day.

Everything else is negotiable.
Nichole Powell

December 30
Over recent years my morning routine has become more tight and focused. The older I get, the less time I want to waste.
Mars Dorian

December 31
Your first ritual that you do during the day is the highest leveraged ritual, by far, because it has the effect of setting your mind, and setting the context, for the rest of your day.
Eben Pagan

Do you like this book?
Please write a review. The link is on the resource page…
Thanks you!

"You'll never change your life until you change something you do daily. The secret of your success is found in your daily routine."
John C. Maxwell

About Frank S. Ring

Frank S. Ring is the author of *Walking for Health and Fitness, The Easiest Way to Get in Shape and Stay in Shape.*

In his second book, *Fitness Walking and Bodyweight Exercises, Supercharge Your Fitness, Build Body Strength, and Live Longer.* Frank has combined his love of walking with the benefits of performing bodyweight fitness exercises as a way to supercharge your fitness.

Frank is a high school teacher and cross-country coach with 21 years of experience. "Teaching is both a rewarding and humbling experience. I gain as much knowledge from my students as they receive from me. I'm like a broken record to my students… 'read more and take action!' All the knowledge in the world won't help you if you fail to act upon it."

In 2016 he began walking as a way to rehab from a back injury and to his great surprise fell in love with walking.

Frank has also combined his love of walking and writing with a website: www.walkingforhealthandfitness.com

"I wanted to share my story, pass along my knowledge, motivate, and inspire others. Walking has brought me back to good health and fitness. I know I can teach others about this great fitness activity."

Frank credits walking with reenergizing his love of teaching and his commitment to staying in great physical condition.

"We all need a lift each day and by reading the quotes in this book and acting on the monthly lessons, I've begun to hit my stride as a parent, husband, author, teacher, coach, and as a man."

Did You Like This Book?
Let everyone know by **posting a review** on Amazon. A link is on the resource page **(Thank You ;-)**

Follow my Author page on Amazon:
Frank S. Ring: www.amazon.com/author/frankring
Receive notices of new book releases, blog and video posts.

Questions or Comments:
Have a question you need to be answered or a comment about the contents of the book or any grammar, proofreading, or formatting issues I should clear up for the next version. Please feel free to email me directly:
Frank@walkingforhealthandfitness.com

More Books By Frank Ring

Book #1: Walking for Health and Fitness

Imagine my surprise when walking solved my major health problem!

Are you like me? Or, should I say like I was in the recent past.

Injured again from running, not exercising due to the injury, my body not recovering as quickly as it did when I was younger, and feeling a little depressed.

I needed help to get in shape during the rehab from my back injury.

I found walking is the easiest way to get in shape and stay in shape.

Why should you be enthusiastic about *Walking for Health and Fitness*?

- Walking is free.
- Walking is easy to do.
- Walking is easy on your muscles, joints, and bones!

Walking for Health and Fitness gives you specific steps to take to get moving today and keep you moving well into the future. Its 170-pages were designed to be read quickly, highlight the benefits of walking, and most importantly... get you out the door walking!

Each of its 22 chapters ends with "Your Next Step"; a very simple plan-of-action to follow as you begin your walking exercise.

Discover the benefits of listening to audiobooks with the FREE DOWNLOAD of the *Walking for Health and Fitness Audiobook*.

An investment in yourself!
Doctor's visits, lost time at work, and the lessened quality of life due to preventable illness all add up to a significant sum of time and money.
This book is an investment in yourself! What could be better than that? Your health, happiness, and life depend on it!

Book #2: Fitness Walking and Bodyweight Exercises
Are You Ready to Learn the Secret to:
Feeling great, living longer, having a positive mindset, and save money in the process?

You need to get in shape and you want to feel good physically and mentally, but you don't know how to start a fitness walking exercise program.

You may have joined a gym to get in shape only to be disillusioned:
You were "turned off" by:
- working out in front of other people
- the gym staff was always pushing you to sign up for expensive personal training sessions
- or, worse of all, the workouts were so far above your fitness level you were injured and couldn't work out for weeks afterward

* * *

Learn about the benefits of walking, and more specifically, the benefits of using fitness walking bodyweight exercises to supercharge your health and fitness while you walk.

Walk and listen to the FREE AUDIOBOOK, it's the ultimate in multitasking.
Bodyweight exercises allow you to control the workout, time you walk, exercises you do, and when and where you work out.

You'll also tap into your mindset at the same time.

Do you know:
- The Core-Four exercises
- How to take control of your fitness
- Why setting goals is a must
- What's your "why?"
- Benefits of bodyweight exercises
- The advantages of bodyweight training
- How to develop a positive mindset
- How exercise improves brain power
- Why diets don't work but my Win-Win strategy does

Products by Walking for Health and Fitness

1. Mindful Walking Exercise Program:
MAKE THE MIND-BODY CONNECTION
Congratulations! You've taken the first step, literally, in your Pleasure Walking exercise journey.

Walking will open up your world to so many new experiences, places to explore, people to see, and adventures to undertake!

And, all this may happen just walking around your neighborhood with a fresh eye on what pleasure walking can bring to your life.

Walking is also the most laid-back exercise you can do, stress-free, fresh air, and peaceful.

Feeling great has never been this easy!

Check out the program at:
https://www.walkingforhealthandfitness.com/pleasure-walking-exercise-program

2. Fitness Walking Exercise Program:
PERFECT FOR BEGINNERS
If I can show you how you can save money and get in great shape in just 35-minutes per day, would you like to learn

more?

Fitness Walking and Bodyweight Exercise Program was designed for both the **beginner** and **experienced walker**.

I'm sharing this with you because studies published in both the Journal of the American Heart Association and The Lancet concluded that a person who exercises five times per week paid **$2,500 less in annual health care expenses** related to heart disease than someone who did not walk or otherwise move for 30 minutes per day, five times per week!
Check out the program at:
https://www.walkingforhealthandfitness.com/fitness-walking-exercise-program

3. Walking for Health and Fitness Complete Program:
Check out the program at:
https://www.walkingforhealthandfitness.com/the-walking-program

Social Media

Follow **Walking for Health and Fitness** and get more information on the many benefits of walking! Also, contribute your story to our social media platforms!

	Walking for Health and Fitness Program
	Walking for Health and Fitness
	WalkingManFrank
	Walking for Health and Fitness
	Walking for Health and Fitness
	Walking for Health and Fitness
	Walking for Health and Fitness

Download our *Get out the Door Checklist* and *Walking Inspiration* our quarterly newsletter completely free.

Bookmark our website: https://www.walkingforhealthandfitness.com

Thank You!

Thank you for purchasing *Walking Inspiration*. It is my sincerest wish that you find the information as inspiring as I have.

Thank you for allowing me to share my belief that walking is the easiest way to get in shape and stay in shape.

I began walking as a way to recover from a serious back injury and absolutely fell in love with this awesome exercise.

I promise if you follow the advice in this book, walking will lead you to good health, fitness, happiness, adventure and most importantly, a journey inward that will change your life!

Walk on,
Frank S. Ring

Did You Like This Book? Let everyone know by posting a review on Amazon.
Download bonus content and click the review link (Thank You ;-)
https://www.walkingforhealthandfitness.com/walking-inspiration-book-resources